KU-674-120

Living Letters

The Paraphrased Epistles

by Kenneth N. Taylor

Printed in USA

PREFACE

God promised that his Word would be "quick, and powerful, and sharper than any two-edged sword." Every generation of believers must communicate the message of the Gospel to its contemporaries. When Paul wrote his letters, he used the language of the common man, the koiné.

As I began to read LIVING LETTERS, it occurred to me that here was something fresh, a paraphrase of the New Testament letters that speaks the language of the hour. I read with renewed interest and inspiration the age-abiding truths of the Scriptures, as though they had come to me direct from the Lord. Then I began to receive reports from some friends who had also shared this experience. We were convinced that this was the blessing and inspiration that we wanted our friends across the nation to enjoy.

The Psalmist said, "The entrance of thy word giveth light." In an hour when spiritual darkness is so evident and when some say that the Gospel is irrelevant, it is thrilling to read the Word with the sense of the eternal, coupled with a style that reads much like today's newspaper. I believe that these paraphrased epistles communicate the message of Christ to our generation. I pray that your reading them will deepen your spiritual life and give you a new understanding of the Scriptures.

Billy Graham

From Wm. Tyndale's Prologue to the First Printed English New Testament: .

Exhortlynge instantly and besechynge those that are better sene in the tongues than I, and that have higher gifts of grace to interpret the sense of Scripture, and meaning of the Spirit, than I, to consider and ponder my labor, and that with the spirit of meekness. And if they perceive in any places that I have not attained the very sense of the tongue, or meaning of the Scripture, or have not given the right English word, that they put to their hands to amend it, remembering that so is their duty to do. For we have not received the gifts of God for ourselves only, or for to hide them; but for to bestow them unto the honoring of God and Christ and edifying of the congregation, which is the body of Christ.

CONTENTS

Romans

CHAPTER 1

Dear Friends in Rome,

1 This letter is from Paul, Jesus Christ's slave, chosen to be a missionary, and sent out to preach God's Good News.

2 This Good News was promised long ago by God's prophets in the Old Testament;

3 It is the Good News about His Son, Jesus Christ our Lord, Who came as a human baby, for He was born into King David's royal family line;

4 And by rising from the dead He proved Himself to be the mighty Son of God, with the holy nature of God Himself.

5 And now, through Christ, all the kindness of God has been poured out upon us undeserving sinners, and now He is sending us out around the world to tell all people everywhere the great things God has done for them, so that they too will believe and obey Him.

6, 7 And you, dear friends in Rome, are among those He dearly loves; you, too, are invited to be His very own—yes, His holy people. May all God's mercies and peace be yours from God our Father and from Jesus Christ our Lord.

8 Let me say first of all that wherever I go I hear you being talked about! For your faith in God is becoming known around the world. How I thank God through

Jesus Christ for this good report, and for each one of you.

9 God knows how often I pray for you. Day and night I bring you and your needs in prayer to the One I serve with all my might, telling others the Good News about His Son.

10 And one of the things I keep on praying for is the opportunity, God willing, to come at last to see you and if possible that I will have a safe trip.

11 For I long to see you so that I can bring you some spiritual food that will help you grow strong in the Lord.

12 Then, too, I need your help, for I not only want to share my faith with you but be encouraged by yours. In that way each of us will be a blessing to the other.

13 I want you to know, dear brothers, that I planned to come many times before (but God did not let me) to work among you and see good results, as I have among the other Gentile churches.

14 For I owe a great debt to you and to everyone else, both to civilized peoples and heathen nations; yes, to the educated and uneducated alike.

15 So, to the fullest extent of my ability, I am ready to come to you in Rome also to preach God's Good News.

16 For I am not ashamed of this Good News about Christ. It is God's powerful method of bringing all who believe it to heaven. This message was preached first to the Jews alone, but now everyone is invited to come to God in this same way.

17 This Good News tells us that God makes us ready for heaven—good in His eyes—when we put

our faith and trust in Christ to save us. And the more we trust Him the more clearly we can see† that He has taken away our sins and filled us with His goodness. As the Old Testament says it, the man who finds life will find it through trusting God.

18 But God shows His anger from heaven against all sinful, evil men who push away the truth.

19 For the truth about God is known to them by instinct; God has put this knowledge in their hearts.

20 Since earliest times men have seen the earth and sky and all God made, and have known of His existence and great eternal power. So they have no excuse for saying they don't know whether or not there is a God.

21 Yes, they knew about Him all right, but they wouldn't admit it or worship Him or even thank Him for all His daily care. And after a while they began to think up silly ideas of what God was like and what He wanted them to do. The result was that their foolish minds became dark and confused.

22 Claiming themselves to be wise without God, they became utter fools instead.

23 And then instead of worshiping the glorious, ever-living God, they took wood and stone and made idols for themselves, carving them to look like birds and animals and snakes and puny men, and said that these were the great, eternal God, and worshiped them.

24 And so God let them go ahead into every sort

†literally: "(this) righteousness of God is *revealed* from faith to faith," i.e., we see ever more clearly what God has done for us, step by step, as our faith grows stronger.

of sex sin, and do whatever they wanted to; yes, vile and sinful things with each other's bodies.

25 Instead of believing what they knew was the truth about God, they deliberately chose to believe lies. So they prayed to the things God made, but wouldn't obey the blessed God who made these things.

26 That is why God let go of them and let them do all these evil things, so that even their women turned against God's natural plan for them and indulged in sex sin with each other.

27 And the men, instead of having a normal sex relationship with women, burned with lust for each other, men doing shameful things with other men and, as a result, getting paid within their own souls with the wages they so richly deserved.

28 So it was that when they gave God up and would not even acknowledge Him, God gave them up to doing everything their evil minds could think of.

29 Their lives became full of every kind of wickedness and sin, of greed and hate, envy, murder, fighting, lying, bitterness, and gossip.

30 They were backbiters, haters of God, insolent, proud braggarts, always thinking of new ways of sinning and continually disobedient to their parents.

31 They tried to misunderstand, broke their promises, and were heartless—without pity.

32 They were fully aware of God's death penalty for these crimes, yet they went right ahead and did them anyway, and encouraged others to do them, too.

CHAPTER 2

Well," you may be saying, "what terrible people you have been talking about!" But wait a minute! You are just as bad. When you say they are wicked and should be punished, you are talking about yourself, for you do these very same things.

2 And we know that God, in justice, will punish anyone who does such things as these.

3 Do you think that God will judge and condemn others for doing them and overlook you when you do them, too?

4 Don't you realize how patient He is being with you? Or don't you care? Can't you see that He has been waiting all this time without punishing you to give you time to turn from your sin? His kindness is meant to lead you to repentance.

5 But no, you won't listen; and so you are saving up terrible punishment for yourselves because of your stubborn hardness of heart, for there is going to come a day of wrath when God will be the honest Judge of all.

6 He will give each one whatever payment he deserves.

7 He will give eternal life to those who patiently do the will of God, seeking for glory and honor and for eternal life.

8 But He will terribly punish those who fight against the truth of God and walk in evil ways, for God's anger will be poured out upon them.

9 There will be sorrow and suffering for Jews and Gentiles alike who keep on sinning.

10 But there will be glory and honor and peace from God for all who obey Him, whether they are Jews or Gentiles.

11 For God treats everyone the same.

12-15 He will punish sin, wherever it is found. He will punish the heathen when they sin, even though they never had God's written laws, for down in their heart they know right from wrong. God's laws are written within them; their own conscience accuses them, or sometimes excuses them. And God will punish the Jews for sinning because they have His written laws but don't obey them. They know what is right but don't do it. After all, salvation is not given to those who know what to do, unless they do it.

16 The day will surely come when at God's command Jesus Christ will judge the secret lives of everyone, their inmost thoughts and motives; this is all part of God's great plan which I have already told you about.

17 You Jews think all is well between yourselves and God because He gave His laws to you; you brag that you are His special friends.

18 Yes, you know what He wants; you know right from wrong and favor the right because you have been taught His laws from earliest youth.

19 You are so sure of the way to God that you could point it out to a blind man. You think of yourselves as beacon lights, directing men to God.

20 You think that you can guide the simple and teach even children the affairs of God, for you really know His laws, which are full of all knowledge and truth.

21 Yes, you teach others—then why don't you teach yourselves? You tell others not to steal—do *you* steal?

22 You say it is wrong to commit adultery—do *you* do it? You say, "Don't pray to idols," but you rob idol temples, which is just as bad.

23 You are so proud of knowing God's laws, *but you dishonor Him by breaking them.*

24 No wonder, as the Scriptures say, the world hates God because of you.

25 Being a Jew is worth something if you obey God's laws, but if you don't, then you are no better off than the heathen.

26 And if the heathen obey God's laws, won't God give them all the rights and honors He planned to give the Jews?

27 In fact, those heathen will be much better off than you Jews who know so much about God and have His promises but don't obey His laws.

28 For you are not real Jews just because you were born of Jewish parents or because you have gone through the Jewish initiation ceremony of circumcision.

29 No, a real Jew is anyone whose heart is right with God. For God is not looking for those who cut their bodies in actual body circumcision, but He is looking for those with changed hearts and minds. Whoever has that kind of change in his life will get his praise from God, even if not from you.

CHAPTER 3

Then what's the use of being a Jew? Are there any special benefits for them from God? Is there any value in the Jewish circumcision ceremony?

2 Yes, being a Jew has many advantages. First of all, God trusted them with His laws (so that they could know and do His will).

3 True, some of them were unfaithful, but just because they broke their promises to God, does that mean God will break His promises to those who love Him?

4 Of course not! Though everyone else in the world is a liar, God is not. Do you remember what the book of Psalms says about this? That God's words will always prove true and right, no matter who questions them.

5 "But," some say, "our breaking faith with God is good, our sins serve a good purpose, for people will notice how good God is when they see how bad we are. Is it fair, then, for Him to punish us when our sins are helping Him?" (That is the way some people talk.)

6 God forbid! Then what kind of God would He be, to overlook sin? How could He ever condemn anyone?

7 For He could not judge and condemn me as a sinner if my dishonesty brought Him glory by pointing up His honesty in contrast to my lies.

8 If you follow through with that idea you come to this: the worse we are, the better God likes it! But the damnation of those who say such things is just. Yet some claim that this is what I preach!

9 Well, then, are we Jews *better* than others? No, not at all, for we have already shown that all men alike are sinners, whether Jews or Gentiles.

10 As the Scriptures say, No one is good—no one in all the world.

11 No one has ever really known God's way, or even truly wanted to.

12 Every one has sinned; all are worthless to God. No one anywhere has kept on doing what is right; not one.

13 Their talk is foul and filthy like the stench from an open grave. Their tongues are loaded with lies. Everything they say has in it the sting and poison of deadly snakes.

14 Their mouths are full of cursing and bitterness.

15 They are quick to kill, hating anyone who disagrees with them.

16 Wherever they go they leave misery and trouble behind them,

17 And they have never known what it is to try to be kind and good.

18 They care nothing about God nor what He thinks of them.

19 So the curse of God lies very heavily upon the Jews, for they are responsible to keep God's laws instead of doing all these evil things; not one of them has any excuse; in fact, all the world stands hushed and guilty before Almighty God.

20 So you can see that no one can ever find God's favor by being good enough. For the more we know of God's laws, the clearer it becomes that we don't obey them, for His laws make us see that we are sinners.

21, 22 But now God has shown us a different way to heaven—not by being "good enough" and trying to keep His laws, but by a new way (though not new, really, for the Old Testament told about it long ago). Now God says He will accept us and make us good and bring us to heaven if we trust Jesus Christ to take away our sins. And we all can be saved in this same way, by coming to Christ, no matter who we are or what we have been like.

23 Yes, all have sinned; all fall short of God's glorious ideal;

24 Yet now God declares that we are good in His eyes if we trust in Jesus Christ, Who freely takes away our sins.

25 For God sent Christ Jesus to take the punishment for our sins and end all God's anger against us. He used Christ's blood and our faith to satisfy God's wrath. In this way He was being entirely fair, even though He did not punish those who sinned in olden times. For He was looking forward to the time when Christ would come and take away those sins.

26 And now in these days also He can receive sinners in this same way, because Jesus took away their sins. But isn't this unfair for God to let criminals go free, and say that they are good? No, for He does it on the basis of their trust in Jesus Who took away their sins.

27 Then what can we boast about doing to earn our salvation? Nothing at all. Why? Because our salvation is not based on our good deeds; it is based on what Christ has done and our faith in Him.

28 So it is that we are saved by faith in Christ and not by the good things we do.

29 And does God save only the Jews in this way? No, the Gentiles, too, may come to Him in this same manner.

30 God treats us all the same; all, whether Jews or Gentiles, are approved if they have faith.

31 Well then, if we are saved by faith, does this mean that we no longer need obey God's laws? That's what it does NOT mean. In fact, only when we trust Jesus can we truly obey Him.

CHAPTER 4

Abraham was, humanly speaking, the founder of our Jewish nation. What were his experiences concerning this question of being saved by faith? Was it because of his good deeds that God accepted him? If so, then he would have something to boast about. But from God's point of view Abraham had no basis at all for pride.

3 For the Scriptures tell us Abraham *believed God,* and that is why God canceled his sins and declared him just and righteous.

4, 5 But didn't he earn his right to heaven by all the good things he did? No, for being saved is a gift; if a person could earn it by being good, then it wouldn't be free—but it is! It is *given* to those who do *not* work for it. For God declares sinners to be good in His sight if they have faith in Christ to save them from God's wrath.

6 King David spoke of this, describing the happiness of an undeserving sinner who is declared good by God.

7 "Blessed, and to be envied," he said, "are those whose sins are forgiven and put out of sight.

8 "Yes, what joy there is for anyone whose sins are no longer counted against him."

9 Now then, the question: Is this blessing given only to those who have faith in Christ but also keep the Jewish laws, or is the blessing also given to those who do not keep the Jewish rules, but only trust in Christ? Well, what about Abraham? We say that he received these blessings through his faith. Was it by faith alone? Or because he also kept the Jewish rules?

10 For the answer to that question, answer this one: *When* did God give this blessing to Abraham? It was *before he became a Jew*—before he went through the Jewish initiation ceremony of circumcision.

11 It wasn't until later on, *after* God had promised to bless him *because of his faith,* that he was circumcised. The circumcision ceremony was a sign that Abraham already had faith and that God had already accepted him and declared him just and good in His sight—before the ceremony took place. So Abraham is an example of those who believe and are saved without obeying Jewish laws. We see, then, that those who do not keep these rules are justified by God through faith.

12 And those who follow these rules and customs and have been circumcised can see that it is not this ceremony that saves them, for Abraham found favor with God by faith alone, before he was circumcised.

13 So it is clear that God's promise to give the whole earth to Abraham and his descendants was not because Abraham obeyed God's laws but because he trusted God to keep His promise.

14 But if you still claim that God's blessings go to those who are "good enough," then you are saying that God's promises to those who have faith are meaningless, and faith is foolish.

15 But the fact of the matter is this: when we try to gain God's blessing and salvation by keeping His laws, we always end up under His anger, for we always fail to keep them. The only way we can keep from breaking laws is not to have any to break!

16 So God's blessings are given to us by faith, as a free gift; we are certain to get them whether or not we follow Jewish customs, if we have faith like Abraham's, for Abraham is the father of us all when it comes to these matters of faith.

17 That is what the Scriptures mean when they say that God made Abraham the father of many nations. God will accept all people in every nation who trust God as Abraham did. And this promise is from God Himself, Who makes the dead live again and speaks of future events with as much certainty as though they were already past!

18 So, when God told Abraham that He would give him a son who would have many children and become a great nation, Abraham believed God even though such a promise just couldn't come to pass!

19 And because his faith was strong, he didn't worry about the fact that he was far too old to be a father, at the age of one hundred, and that Sarah his wife, at ninety,† was also much too old to have a baby.

20 But Abraham never doubted. He believed God, for his faith and trust were strong, and he praised God for this blessing before it even happened.

21 He was completely sure that God was well able to do anything He promised.

†Genesis 17:17

22 And because of Abraham's faith God forgave his sins and called him just and good.

23 Now this wonderful promise—that he was accepted and approved through his faith—wasn't just for Abraham's benefit.

24 It was for us, too, assuring us that God will accept us in the same way He accepted Abraham—when we believe the promises of God Who brought back Jesus our Lord from the dead.

25 He died for our sins and rose again to make us right with God, filling us with God's goodness.

CHAPTER 5

So, now, since we have been made right in God's sight by faith in His promises, we can have real peace with Him because of what Jesus Christ our Lord has done for us.

2 For because of our faith, He has brought us into this place of highest privilege where we now stand, and we confidently and joyfully look forward to actually becoming all that God has had in mind for us to be.

3 We can rejoice, too, when we run into problems and trials for we know that they are good for us—they help us learn to be patient.

4 And patience develops strength of character in us and helps us trust God more each time until finally our hope and faith are strong and steady.

5 Then, when that happens, we will be able to hold our heads high no matter what happens and know that all is well, for we will know how dearly God loves us, and we will feel this warm love everywhere within

us because God has given us the Holy Spirit to fill our hearts with His love.

6 When we were utterly helpless with no way of escape, Christ came at just the right time and died for us sinners who had no use for Him.

7 Even if we were good, we really wouldn't expect anyone to die for us, though of course that might be barely possible.

8 But God showed His great love for us by sending Christ to die for us while we were still sinners.

9 And since by His blood He did all this for us as sinners, how much more will He do for us now that He has declared us just and good? Now He will save us from all of God's wrath to come.

10 And since, when we were His enemies we were brought back to God by the death of His Son, what blessings He must have for us now that we are His friends, and He is living within us!

11 Now we have the wonderful joy of the Lord in our lives because of what our Lord Jesus Christ has done in dying for our sins and making us His friends.

12 When Adam sinned the entire human race was declared guilty. His sin brought death into the world, and so everything began to grow old and die.

13 (We know that it was Adam's sin that caused this—and not each person dying because of his own sins—because although of course people were sinning from the time of Adam until Moses, God did not in those days judge them guilty of death for breaking His laws—because He had not yet given His laws to them, nor told them what He wanted them to do.

14 So when they died it was not for these sins of

their own; and since they themselves had never disobeyed God's special law against eating the forbidden fruit, as Adam had, their dying was not because of that. It was because, when Adam sinned, all of us were declared guilty with him and began to die because of his sin.) What a contrast between Adam and Christ Who was yet to come.

15 And what a difference between man's sin and God's forgiveness. For this one man, Adam, brought death to many through his *sin*. But this one man, Jesus Christ, brought forgiveness to many through God's *mercy*.

16 Adam's *one* sin brought the penalty of death to many, while Christ freely takes away *many* sins and gives glorious life instead.

17 The sin of this one man, Adam, caused *death to be king over all*, but all who will take God's gift of forgiveness and approval are *kings of life* because of this one man, Jesus Christ.

18 Yes, Adam's *sin* brought *punishment* to all, but Christ's act of *goodness* makes men *right with God*, so that they can live.

19 Adam caused many to be sinners because he *disobeyed* God, and Christ caused many to be made acceptable to God because He *obeyed*.

20 The Ten Commandments were given so that all could see the extent of their failure to obey God's laws. But the more we see our sinfulness, the more we see God's abounding grace forgiving us.

21 And so sin ruled over all men and brought them to death, but now God's kindness rules instead, giving

us right standing with God and resulting in eternal life through Jesus Christ our Lord.

CHAPTER 6

Well then, shall we keep on sinning so that God can keep on showing us more and more kindness and forgiveness?

2, 3 Of course not! Should we keep on sinning when we don't have to? For sin's power over us was broken when we became Christians and were baptized to become a part of Jesus Christ: through His death the power of your sinful nature was shattered.

4 Your old sin-loving nature was buried with Him by baptism when He died, and when God the Father, with glorious power, brought Him back to life again, you were given His wonderful new life to enjoy.

5 For you have become a part of Him, and so you died with Him, so to speak, when He died; and now you share His new life, for you have risen with Him when He rose.

6 Your old evil desires were nailed to the cross with Him; that part of you that loves to sin was crushed and fatally wounded, so that your sin-loving body is no longer under sin's control, no longer needs to be a slave to sin;

7 For when you are deadened to sin you are freed from all its allure and its power over you.

8 And since your old sin-loving nature "died" with Christ, we believe that you are now sharing His new life.

9 Christ rose from the dead and will never die again. Death no longer has any power over Him.

10 He died once for all to end sin's power, but now He lives forever in unbroken fellowship with God.

11 So look upon your old sin nature as dead and unresponsive to sin and be alive instead to God, alert to Him, through Jesus Christ our Lord.

12 Do not let sin control you any longer; do not obey it; do not submit to it by giving in to its desires.

13 Do not let any part of your bodies become tools of wickedness, to be used for sinning; but give yourselves completely to God—every part of you—for you are back from death and you want to be tools in the hands of God, to be used for His good purposes.

14 Sin need never again be your master, for now you are no longer tied to the law where sin enslaves you, but you are free under God's favor and mercy.

15 So now shall we sin and not worry about it? (For our salvation does not depend on keeping the law, but on receiving God's grace!) Of course not!

16 Don't you realize that you can choose your own master? You can choose sin (with death) or else obedience (with goodness). The one to whom you offer yourself, he will take you and be your master and you will be his slave.

17 Thank God that though you once chose to be slaves of sin, now you are obeying with all your heart the teaching to which God has committed you.

18 And now you are free from your old master, sin; and you have become slaves to your new master, goodness and righteousness.

19 I speak this way, using the illustration about slaves, because it makes it easy to understand: just as

you used to be slaves to all kinds of sin, so now you must let yourselves be slaves to all that is right and holy.

20 In those days when you were slaves of sin you didn't bother much with goodness.

21 And what was the result? Evidently not good, since you are ashamed now even to think about those things you used to do, for they ruined you.

22 But now you are free from the power of sin and are slaves of God, and His benefits to you include holiness and everlasting life.

23 For the wages of sin is death, but the free gift of God is eternal life through Jesus Christ our Lord.

CHAPTER 7

Don't you understand yet, dear Jewish brothers in Christ, that when a person dies the law no longer holds him in its power?

2 Let me illustrate: when a woman marries, the law binds her to her husband as long as he is alive. But if he dies, she is no longer bound to him. The laws of marriage no longer apply to her.

3 Then she can marry someone else if she wants to. That would be wrong while he was alive, but it is perfectly all right after he dies.

4 Your "husband," your master, used to be the Jewish law; but you "died," as it were, with Christ on the cross; and since you are "dead," you are no longer "married to the law," and it has no more power over you. Then you came back to life again when Christ did, and are a new person. And now you are "married," so

to speak, to the One who rose from the dead, so that you can produce good fruit, that is, good deeds for God.

5 When your old nature was still active, sinful desires were at work within you, making you want to do whatever God said not to, and producing sinful deeds, the rotting fruit that comes with death.

6 But now you need no longer worry about the Jewish laws and customs because you "died" while in their captivity, and now you can really serve God; not in the old way, mechanically obeying a set of rules, but in the new way, with all of your hearts and minds.

7 Well then, am I suggesting that these laws of God are evil? Of course not! No, the law is not sinful but it was the law that showed me my sin. I would never have known the sin in my heart—the evil desires that are hidden there—except the law said, "You must not have evil desires in your heart."

8 But sin used this law against evil desires by reminding me that such desires are wrong and arousing all kinds of forbidden desires within me! Only if there were no laws to break would there be no sinning.

9 That is why I felt fine so long as I did not understand what the law really demanded. But when I found out then I realized that I had broken the law and was a sinner, doomed to die.

10 So as far as I was concerned, the good law which was supposed to show me the way of life resulted instead in my being given the death penalty.

11 Sin fooled me by taking the good laws of God and using them to make me guilty of death.

12 So you see the law itself is wholly right and good.

13 But didn't the law cause my doom? How then can it be good? No, it was sin, devilish stuff that it is, that used what was good to bring about my condemnation. So you can see from the way sin uses God's good laws for its own evil purposes, how cunning and deadly and damnable it is.

14 The law is good. The trouble is not there, but with *me,* because I am too sinful to obey it.

15 I don't understand myself at all, for I really want to do what is right, but I can't. I do what I don't want to—what I hate.

16 I know perfectly well that what I am doing is wrong and that the laws I am breaking are good ones.

17 But I can't help myself because I'm not doing it. It is sin inside me that is stronger than I am that makes me do these evil things.

18 I know I am rotten through and through so far as my old sinful nature is concerned. No matter which way I turn I can't make myself do right. I want to but I can't.

19 When I want to do good, I don't; and when I try not to do wrong, I do it anyway.

20 Now if I am doing what I don't want to, it is plain where the trouble is: sin still has me in its evil grasp.

21 It seems to be a fact of life that when I want to do what is right, I inevitably do what is wrong.

22 I love to do God's will so far as my new nature is concerned;

23 But there is something else deep within me, in my lower nature, that is at war with my mind and wins the fight and makes me a slave to the sin and death that

are still within me. In my mind I want to be God's willing servant but instead I find myself still enslaved to sin.

24, 25 So you see how it is: my new life tells me to do right, but the old nature that is still inside me loves to sin. Oh, what a terrible thing this is! Who will free me from my slavery to this deadly lower nature? Thank God! It has been done through Jesus Christ our Lord. He has set me free.

CHAPTER 8

So there is no condemnation awaiting those who belong to Christ Jesus.

2 For the power of the life-giving Spirit—and this power is mine through Christ Jesus—has freed me from the vicious circle of sin and death.

3 We aren't saved from sin's grasp by knowing the commandments of God, because we can't and don't keep them, but God put into effect a different plan to save us. He sent His own Son, in a human body like ours—except that ours are sinful—and destroyed sin's control over us by giving Himself as a sacrifice for our sins.

4 So now we can obey God's laws if we follow after the Holy Spirit and no longer obey the old evil nature within us.

5 Those who let themselves be controlled by their lower natures live only to please themselves; but those who follow after the Holy Spirit find themselves doing those things that please God.

6 Following after the Holy Spirit leads to life and peace, but following after the old nature leads to death,

7 Because the old sinful nature within us is against God. It never did obey God's laws and it never will.

8 That's why those who are still under the control of their old sinful selves, bent on following their old evil desires, can never please God.

9 But you are not like that. You are controlled by your new nature if you have the Spirit of God living in you. (And remember that if anyone doesn't have the Spirit of Christ living in him, he is not a Christian at all.)

10 Yet, even though Christ lives within you, your body will die because of sin; but your spirit will live, for Christ has made it just and good.

11 And if the Spirit of God, Who raised up Jesus from the dead, lives in you, He will make your dying bodies live again after you die, by means of this same Holy Spirit living within you.

12 So, dear brothers, you have no obligations whatever to your old sinful nature to do what it begs you to do.

13 For if you keep on following it you are lost and will perish, but if through the power of the Holy Spirit you crush it and its evil deeds, you will live.

14 For all who are led by the Spirit of God are sons of God.

15 And so we should not be like cringing, fearful slaves, but we should behave like God's very own children, adopted into the bosom of His family, and calling to Him, "Father, Father."

16 For His Holy Spirit speaks to us deep in our hearts, and tells us that we really are God's children.

17 And since we are His children, then we will share His treasures—for all God gives His Son Jesus is ours now too. But we must also share His suffering if we are to share His glory.

18 Yet what we suffer now is nothing compared to the glory He will give us later.

19 For all creation is waiting patiently and hopefully for that future day when God will glorify His children.†

20, 21 For on that day thorns and thistles, sin, death, and decay that overcame the world against its will at God's command will all disappear, and the world around us will share in the glorious freedom from sin which God's children enjoy.

22 For we know that even the things of nature, like animals and plants, groan in sickness and death as they await this great event.

23 And even we Christians, although we have the witness of the Holy Spirit within us, aren't free from trouble; we too wait anxiously for that day when God will give us our full rights as His children, including the new bodies He has promised us—bodies that will not be sick again and that will never die.

24 We are saved by trusting. And trusting means looking forward to getting something we don't have now; (for a man who already has something doesn't need to hope and trust that he will get it.)

25 But if we must keep trusting God for something that hasn't happened yet, it teaches us to wait patiently and confidently.

†literally: "waiting for the revelation of the sons of God"

26 And in the same way—by faith—the Holy Spirit helps us with our daily problems and in our praying. For we don't even know what we should pray for, nor how to pray as we should; but the Holy Spirit prays for us with such feeling that it cannot be expressed in words.

27 And the Father Who knows all hearts knows of course what the Spirit is saying as He pleads for us in harmony with God's own will.

28 And we know that all that happens to us is working for our good if we love God, and if we are fitting into His plans.

29 For from the very beginning God decided that those who came to Him—and all along He knew who would—should become like His Son, so that His Son would be the first, with many brothers.

30 And having chosen us, He called us to come to Him; and when we came, He declared us "not guilty," filled us with Christ's goodness, gave us right standing with Himself, and promised us His glory.

31 What can we ever say to such wonderful things as these? If God is on our side, who can ever be against us?

32 Since He did not even spare His own Son for us but gave Him up for us all, won't He also surely give us everything else?

33 Who dares accuse us whom God has chosen for His own? Will God? No! He is the One Who has forgiven us and given us right standing with Himself.

34 Who then will condemn us? Will Christ? NO! For He is the One Who died for us and came back to life again for us and is sitting at the place of highest

honor next to God, pleading for us there in heaven.

35 Who then can ever keep away Christ's love from us? When we have trouble or calamity, when we are hunted down or destroyed, is it because He doesn't love us anymore? And if we are hungry, or penniless, or in danger, or threatened with death, has God deserted us?

36 No, for the Scriptures tell us that for His sake we must be ready to face death at every moment of the day—we are like sheep awaiting slaughter;

37 But despite all this, overwhelming victory is ours through Christ Who loves us.

38 For I am convinced that nothing can ever separate us from His love. Death can't, and life can't. The angels won't, and all the powers of hell itself cannot keep God's love away. Our fears for today, our worries about tomorrow.

39 Or where we are—high above the sky, or in the deepest ocean—nothing will ever be able to separate us from the love of God that is in Christ Jesus, our Lord.

CHAPTER 9

Oh, Israel, my people! Oh, my Jewish brothers! How I long for you to come to Christ. My heart is heavy within me and I grieve bitterly day and night because of you. Christ knows and the Holy Spirit knows that it is no mere pretense when I say that I would be willing to be forever damned if that would save you.

4 God has given you so much, but still you will not listen to Him. He took you as His own special,

chosen people and led you along with a bright cloud of glory and told you how very much He wanted to bless you. He gave you His rules for daily life so you would know what He wanted you to do. He let you work for Him in the temple. He gave you mighty promises.

5 Great men of God were your fathers, and Christ Himself was One of you, a Jew so far as His human nature is concerned, He Who now rules over all things and is blessed of God forever.

6 Well then, did God's promises to His Jewish people become worthless when they refused to come to be saved? Of course not. For His promises are only to those who come. Only they are truly His people. They alone are truly Jews. So you see, not everyone born into a Jewish family is truly a Jew.

7 Just because they come from Abraham doesn't make them truly Abraham's children. For the Scriptures say that the promises apply only to Abraham's son Isaac and Isaac's descendants, though Abraham had other children too.

8 This means that not all of Abraham's children are children of God, but only the ones born as a result of God's special promise to Abraham.

9 For God had promised, "Next year I willl give you and Sarah a son (Isaac)."

10-13 And years later, when Isaac was grown up and married, and Rebecca his wife was about to bear him twin children, God told her that Esau, the child born first, would be a servant to Jacob, his twin brother. In the words of the Scripture, "I chose to bless Jacob, but not Esau." And God said this before the children were even born, before they had done anything either good or bad. This proves that God was doing what He had decided from the beginning; it was not because of what the children did but because of what God wanted and chose.

14 Was God being unfair? Of course not.

15 For God had said to Moses, "If I want to be kind to someone, I will. And I will take pity on anyone I want to."

16 And so God's blessings are not given just because someone decides to have them or works hard to get them. They are given to those God wants to give them to.

17 Pharaoh king of Egypt was an example of this fact. For God told him He had given him the kingdom of Egypt for the very purpose of displaying the awesome power of God against him: so that all the world would hear about God's glorious name.

18 So you see, God is kind to some just because He wants to be, and He makes some refuse to listen.

19 Well then, why does God blame them for not listening? Haven't they done what He made them do?

20 No, don't say that. Who are you to criticize God? Should the thing made say to the One who made it, "Why have you made me like this?"

21 When a man makes a jar out of clay, doesn't he have a right to use the same lump of clay to make one jar beautiful, to be used for holding flowers, and another to throw garbage into?

22 And so God has a perfect right to be patient with whomever He wants to, even with those who are fit only for destruction; later on He will show His fury and power against them.

24 And He has a right to take others such as ourselves, who have been made for pouring His glory into, whether we are Jews or Gentiles, and to be kind to us so that everyone can see how very great His glory is.

25 Remember what it says in the book of Hosea? There God says that He will find other children for Himself (who are not from His Jewish family) and will love them, though no one had ever loved them before.

26 And the heathen of whom it once was said, "You are not my people" shall be called "sons of the Living God."

27 Isaiah the prophet cried out concerning the Jews that though there would be millions† of them, only a small number would ever be saved.

28 For the Lord will execute His sentence upon the earth, quickly ending His dealings, justly cutting them short.

29 And Isaiah says in another place that except for God's mercy all the Jews would be destroyed—all of them—just as everyone in the cities of Sodom and Gomorrah perished.

30 Well then, what shall we say about these things? Just this, that God has given the Gentiles the opportunity to be saved by faith, even though they really were not seeking God.

31 But the Jews, who tried so hard to be right with God by keeping His laws, did not find His salvation.

32 Why not? Because they were trying to be saved by keeping the law and being good instead of by de-

†literally: "as the sand of the sea," *i.e.*, numberless.

pending on faith. They have stumbled over the great stumblingstone.

33 God warned them of this in the Scriptures when He said, "I have put a Rock in the path of the Jews, and many will stumble over Him (Jesus). But those who believe in Him will never be disappointed."

CHAPTER 10

Dear brothers, the longing of my heart and my prayer is that the Jewish people might be saved.

2 I know what enthusiasm you have for the honor of God, but it is misdirected zeal.

3 For you don't understand that Christ has died to make you right with God. Instead you are trying to make yourselves good enough to gain God's favor by keeping the Jewish laws and customs. But that is not God's way of salvation.

4 You don't understand that Christ gives to those who trust in Him everything you are trying to get by keeping His laws.

5 For as Moses said, if a person could be perfectly good and hold out against temptation all his life and never sin once, only then could he be saved.

6 But the salvation that comes through faith says, "You don't need to search the heavens to find Christ and bring Him down to help you," and,

7 "You don't need to go among the dead to bring Christ back to life again,"

8 For salvation that comes from trusting Christ—which is what we preach—is already within easy reach

of each of us; in fact, it is as near as our own hearts and mouths.

9 For if you tell others with your own mouth that Jesus Christ is your Lord, and believe in your own heart that God has raised Him from the dead, you will be saved.

10 For it is by believing in his heart that a man becomes right with God; and with his mouth he tells others of his faith, confirming his salvation.

11 For the Scriptures tell us that no one who believes in Christ will ever be disappointed.

12 Jew and Gentile are the same in this respect: they all have the same Lord Who generously gives His riches to all those who ask Him for them.

13 Anyone who calls upon the name of the Lord will be saved.

14 But how shall they ask Him to save them unless they believe in Him? And how can they believe in Him if they have never heard about Him? And how can they hear about Him unless someone tells them?

15 And how will anyone go and tell them unless someone sends him? That is what the Scriptures are talking about when they say, "How beautiful are the feet of those who preach the Gospel of peace, and bring glad tidings of good things." In other words, how welcome are those who come preaching God's Good News!

16 But not everyone who hears the Good News has welcomed it, for Isaiah the prophet said, "Lord, who has believed me when I told them?"

17 Yet faith comes from listening to this Good

News—the Good News about Christ, Who is the Word of God.

18 But what about the Jews? Have they heard God's word? Yes, for it has gone wherever they are. The Good News has been told to the ends of the earth.

19 And did they know that God would give His salvation to others if they refused to take it? Yes, for even back in the time of Moses, God had said that He would make His people jealous and try to wake them up by giving His salvation to the foolish heathen nations.

20 And later on Isaiah said boldly that God would be found by people who weren't even looking for Him, and they would be saved.

21 In the meantime, He keeps on reaching out His hands to the Jews but they keep arguing and refusing to come.

CHAPTER 11

I ask then, has God rejected and deserted His people the Jews? Oh no, not at all. Remember that I myself am a Jew, a descendant of Abraham and a member of Benjamin's family;

2, 3 No, God has not discarded His own people whom He chose from the very beginning. Do you remember what the Scriptures say about this? Elijah the prophet was complaining to God about the Jews, telling God how they had killed the prophets and torn down God's altars; Elijah claimed that he was the only one left in all the land who still loved God, and now they were trying to kill him too.

4 And do you remember how God replied? God said, "No, you are not the only one left. I have seven thousand others besides you who still love Me and have not bowed down to idols!"

5 It is the same today. Not all the Jews have turned away from God. There are a few being saved as a result of God's kindness in choosing them.

6 And if it is by God's kindness, then it is not by their being good enough. For in that case the free gift would no longer be free—it isn't free when it is earned.

7 So this is the situation: most of the Jews have not found the favor of God they are looking for. A few have, the ones God has picked out, but the eyes of the others have been blinded.

8 This is what our Scriptures refer to when they say that God has put them to sleep, shutting their eyes and ears so that they do not understand what we are talking about when we tell them of Christ. And so it is to this very day.

9 King David spoke of this same thing when he said, "Let their good food and other blessings trap them into thinking all is well between themselves and God. Let these good things boomerang upon them and fall back upon their heads to justly crush them."

10 "Let their eyes be dim," he said, "so that they cannot see, and let them walk bent-backed forever with a heavy load."

11 Did God make His Jewish people stumble like this for the purpose of bringing disaster to them? Oh no, His purpose was to make His salvation available

to the Gentiles, and then the Jews would be jealous and begin to want God's salvation for themselves.

12 Now if the whole world became rich as a result of God's offer of salvation, when the Jews stumbled over it and turned it down, think how much greater a blessing the world will share in later on when the Jews too come to Christ.

13 As you know, God has appointed me as a special messenger to you Gentiles. I lay great stress on this and remind the Jews about it as often as I can,

14 So that if possible I can make them want what you Gentiles have and in that way save some of them.

15 And how wonderful it is when they become Christians. When God turned away from them it meant that He turned to the rest of the world to offer His salvation; and now it is even more wonderful when some of the Jews come to Christ. It is like dead people coming back to life again.

16 And since Abraham and the prophets are God's people, their children will be too. For if the roots of the tree are holy, the branches will be too.

17 But some of these branches from Abraham's tree, some of the Jews, have been broken off. And you Gentiles who were branches from, we might say, a wild olive tree, were grafted in. So now you too receive the blessing God has promised Abraham and his children, sharing in God's rich nourishment of His own special olive tree.

18 But you must be careful not to brag about being put in to replace the branches that were broken off. Remember that you are important only because you are

now a part of God's tree; you are just a branch, not a root.

19 "Well," you may be saying, "those branches were broken off to make room for me so I must be pretty good."

20 Watch out! Remember that those branches, the Jews, were broken off because they didn't believe God, and you are there only because you do. Do not be proud; be humble and grateful—and careful.

21 For if God did not spare the branches He put there in the first place, He won't spare you either.

22 See how God is both so kind and so severe. He is very hard on those who disobey, but very good to you if you continue to love and trust Him. But if you don't, you too will be cut off.

23 On the other hand, if the Jews leave their unbelief behind them and come back to God, God will graft them back into the tree again. He has the power to do it.

24 For if God was willing to take you who were so far away from Him—being part of a wild olive tree—and graft you into His own good tree—a very unusual thing to do—don't you see that He will be far more ready to put the Jews back again, who were there in the first place?

25 I want you to know about this mystery, dear brothers, so that you will not feel proud and start bragging. Yes, it is true that most of the Jews have set themselves against the Gospel now, but this will last only until all of you Gentiles have come to Christ—those of you who will.

26 And then all Israel will be saved. Do you re-

member what the prophets said about this? "There shall come out of Zion a Deliverer, and He shall turn the Jews from all ungodliness.

27 "At that time I will take away their sins, just as I promised."

28 Now most of the Jews are enemies of the Gospel. They hate it. But this has been a benefit to you, for it has resulted in God giving His gifts to you Gentiles. But the Jews are still beloved of God because of His promises to Abraham, Isaac, and Jacob.

29 For God's gifts and His call can never be withdrawn; He will never go back on His promises.

30 Once you were rebels against God, but when the Jews refused His gifts God was merciful to you instead.

31 And now the Jews are the rebels, but some day they will share in God's mercy upon you.

32 For God arranged that all be sinners so that He could have mercy upon all alike.

33 Oh what a wonderful God we have! How great are His wisdom and knowledge and riches. How impossible it is for us to understand His decisions and His methods.

34 For who among us can know the mind of the Lord? Who knows enough to be His counselor and guide?

35 And who has ever given anything to the Lord first as payment for something in return?

36 For everything comes from God alone. Everything lives by His power, and everything is for His glory. To him be glory evermore.

CHAPTER 12

And so, dear brothers, I plead with you to give your bodies to God. Let them be a living sacrifice, holy—the kind He can accept. When you think of what He has done for you, is this too much to ask?

2 Don't copy the fashions and customs of this world, but be a new and different person with a fresh newness in all you do and think. Then you will see from your own experience how His ways will really satisfy you.

3 As God's messenger I give each of you God's warning: be honest in your estimate of yourselves, measuring your value by how much faith God has given you.

4, 5 For just as there are many parts to our bodies, so it is with Christ's body. We are all parts of it, and it takes every one of us to make it complete, for we each have different work to do. So we belong to each other, and each needs all the others.

6 God has given each of us the ability to do certain things well. So if God has given you the ability to prophesy, then prophesy whenever you can—as often as your faith is strong enough to produce a message from God.

7 If your gift is that of serving others, serve them well. Teachers should do a good job of teaching.

8 The preacher should see to it that his sermons are strong and helpful. If God has given you money, be generous in helping others with it. If God has given you administrative ability and put you in charge of the work

of others, take the responsibility seriously. And if yours is the gift of kindness to others, do it cheerfully.

9 Don't just pretend that you love others: really love them. Hate what is wrong. Stand on the side of the good.

10 Love each other with brotherly affection and delight to honor each other.

11 Never be lazy in your work but serve the Lord enthusiastically.

12 Be glad for all God is planning for you. Be patient in trouble, and prayerful always.

13 When God's children are in need, you be the one to help them out. And get into the habit of inviting guests home for dinner; or, if they need lodging, for the night.

14 If someone harms you, don't curse him; pray that God will bless him.

15 When others are happy, be happy with them. If they are sad, share their sorrow.

16 Work happily together. Don't try to act big. Don't try to get into the good graces of important people, but enjoy the company of ordinary folks. And don't think you know it all!

17 Never pay back evil for evil. Do things in such a way that everyone can see you are honest clear through.

18 Don't quarrel with anyone. Be at peace with everyone, just as much as you possibly can.

19 Dear friends, never avenge yourselves. Let anger cool, for God has said that He will pay back those deserving it.

20 So feed your enemy if he is hungry. If he is

thirsty give him something to drink and you will be "heaping coals of fire on his head." In other words, he will feel ashamed of himself for what he has done to you.

21 Don't let evil get the upper hand but conquer evil by doing good.

CHAPTER 13

Obey the government, for God is the One Who has put it there. There is no government anywhere that God has not placed in power.

2 So those who refuse to obey the laws of the land are refusing to obey God, and punishment will follow.

3 For the policeman is not there to frighten people doing right; but those doing evil will always fear him. So if you don't want to be afraid, keep the laws and you will get along well.

4 The policeman is sent by God to help you. But if you are doing something wrong, of course you should be afraid, for he will have you punished. He is sent by God for that very purpose.

5 So you must obey the laws for two reasons: to keep from being punished and because you know you should.

6 Pay your taxes too, for these same two reasons. For government workers need to be paid so that they can keep on doing God's work, serving you.

7 Pay everyone whatever he ought to have: pay your taxes and import duties gladly, obey those over you and give honor and respect to all those to whom it is due.

8 Pay all your debts except the debt of love for others; never finish paying that! For if you love them, you will be obeying all of God's laws, fulfilling all His requirements.

9 If you love your neighbor as much as you love yourself you will not want to harm or cheat him, or kill him or steal from him. And you won't sin with his wife or want what is his, or do anything else the Ten Commandments say are wrong. All ten are wrapped up in this one, to love your neighbor as you love yourself.

10 Love does no wrong to anyone. That's why it fully satisfies all of God's requirements. It is the only law you need.

11 Another reason for right living is this: you know how late it is; time is running out. Wake up, for the coming of the Lord is nearer now than when we first believed.

12 The night is far gone, the day of His return will soon be here. So we must quit the evil deeds of darkness and put on the armor of upright living.

13 We must be honest and true so that all can see that everything we do is good. We are not to spend our time in wild parties and drunkenness, or in adultery and lust, or in fighting, or wishing for things that don't belong to us.

14 But ask the Lord Jesus Christ to help you live as you should and don't make plans to enjoy evil.

CHAPTER 14

Give a warm welcome to any brother who wants to join you as a member of the church, even if he scarce believes that Christ alone can save him. Don't criticize him for having different ideas from yours about what is right and wrong.

2 For instance, don't argue with him about whether or not to eat meat that has been offered to idols. You may believe there is no harm in this, but the faith of others is weaker; they think it is wrong, and will go without any meat at all and eat vegetables rather than eat that kind of meat.

3 Those who think it is all right to eat such meat must not look down on those who won't. And if you are one of those who won't, don't find fault with those who do. For God has accepted them to be His children.

4 They are God's servants, not yours. Let Him tell them what to do. They are responsible to God, not you, and God will help them do what is right.

5 Some think that Christians should observe the Jewish holidays as special days to worship God, but others say it is wrong and foolish to go to all that trouble for every day alike belongs to God. On questions of this kind everyone must decide for himself.

6 If you have special days for worshiping the Lord, you are trying to honor Him; you are doing a good thing. So is the person who eats meat that has been offered to idols; he is thankful to the Lord for it; he is doing right. And the person who won't touch such meat, he too is anxious to please the Lord, and is thankful.

7 We are not our own bosses to live or die as we ourselves might choose.

8 Living or dying we follow the Lord. Living or dying we are His.

9 That is why Christ died and rose again, so that He can be our Lord both while we live and when we die.

10 You have no right to criticize your brother or look down on him. Remember, each of us will stand personally before the Judgment Seat of Christ.

11 For it is written, "As I live," says the Lord, "every knee shall bow to me and every tongue confess to God."

12 Yes, each of us will give an account of himself to God.

13 So don't criticize each other any more. Try instead to live in such a way that you will never make your brother stumble by letting him see you doing something he thinks is wrong.

14 As a matter of fact, I am perfectly sure on the authority of the Lord Jesus that there is nothing really wrong with eating meat that has been offered to idols. But if someone feels it is wrong, then he shouldn't do it for it is wrong for him.

15 If your brother is bothered by what you eat, you are not acting in love if you go ahead and eat it. Don't let your eating ruin someone for whom Christ died.

16 Don't do that which will cause criticism against yourself even though you know that what you do is right.

17 For after all the important thing for us as Christians is not what we eat or drink but stirring up goodness and peace and joy from the Holy Spirit.

18 If you follow Christ's example in these affairs, God will be glad; and so will your friends.

19 So aim for harmony in the church and to build each other up.

20 Don't undo the work of God for a chunk of meat. Remember, there is nothing wrong with the meat but it is wrong to eat it if it makes another stumble.

21 The right thing to do is to quit eating meat or drinking wine or doing anything else that offends your brother or makes him sin by causing resentment or influencing him to do what he feels is wrong.

22 You may know that there is nothing wrong with what you plan, even from God's point of view, but keep it to yourself; don't flaunt your faith in front of others who might be hurt by it. In this situation, happy is the man who does not sin by doing what he knows is right.

23 But anyone who feels it is wrong shouldn't do it. He sins if he does, for he thinks it is wrong; and so for him it is wrong. Anything that's done apart from what he feels is right is sin.

CHAPTER 15

Even if we believe that it makes no difference to the Lord that we do these things, still we cannot just go ahead and do them to please ourselves; for we must bear the "burden" of being considerate of the doubts and fears of others—of those who feel these things are wrong. Let's please the other fellow, not ourselves, if it is for his good and builds him up in the Lord.

3 Christ didn't please Himself. As the prophets said, He came for the very purpose of suffering under the insults of those who were against the Lord.

4 And these things that were written by God so

long ago are to teach us patience and to encourage us, so that we will look expectantly to God for help.

5 May God Who gives patience, steadiness, and encouragement help you to live in full harmony with each other—each with the attitude of Christ toward the other.

6 And then all of us can praise the Lord together with one voice, giving glory to God, the Father of our Lord Jesus Christ.

7 So, warmly welcome each other into the church, just as Christ has warmly welcomed you; then God will be glorified.

8 Remember that Jesus Christ came to help the Jews, so that He could fulfill the promises God made to their ancestors.

9 And remember that the Gentiles give glory to God for His mercies to them. That is what the Psalmist meant when he wrote: "I shall praise You among the Gentiles, and sing to Your name."

10 And in another place, "Be glad, O you Gentiles, along with His people the Jews."

11 And yet again, "Praise the Lord, O you Gentiles, let everyone praise Him."

12 And the prophet Isaiah said, "There shall be an Heir in the house of Jesse, and He will be King over the Gentiles; they will pin their hopes on Him alone."

13 So I pray for you Gentiles that God Who gives you hope will keep you happy and full of peace as you believe in Him. I pray that God will help you overflow with hope in Him through the Holy Spirit's power within you.

14 I know that you are wise and good, my brothers,

and that you know these things so well that you are able to teach others all about them.

15, 16 But even so I have been bold enough to emphasize some of these points, knowing that all you need is this reminder from me; for I am, by God's grace, a special messenger from Jesus Christ to you Gentiles bringing you the Gospel and offering you up as a fragrant sacrifice to God; for you have been made pure and pleasing to Him by the Holy Spirit.

17 So it is right for me to be a little proud of all Christ Jesus has done for you through me.

18 I dare not judge how effectively He has used others, but I know this: He has used me to win the Gentiles to God.

19 I have won them by my message and by the good way I have lived before them, and by miracles done through me as signs from God—all by the Holy Spirit's power. In this way I have preached the full Gospel of Christ all the way from Jerusalem clear over into Illyricum.

20 But my ambition is to go and preach where the name of Christ has never yet been heard, rather than where a church has already been started by someone else.

21 I want to follow the plan spoken of in the Scriptures where Isaiah says that those who have never heard the name of Christ before will see and understand.

22 That is why I have been so long in coming to visit you.

23 But now at last I am through with my work here, and I am ready to come after all these long years of waiting.

24 So when I take the trip to Spain I am planning, I will stop off there in Rome; and after we have had a good time together for a little while, you can start me on my way again.

25 First, though, I must go down to Jerusalem to carry a gift to the Christians there.

26 For you see, the Christians in Macedonia and Achaia have taken up an offering for those in Jerusalem who are going through some hard times.

27 They were very glad to do this, for they feel that they owe a real debt to the Jerusalem Christians. Why? Because the news about Christ came to them from the church in Jerusalem. And since they received this wonderful spiritual gift of the Gospel from them, they feel that the least they can do in return is to give them some food!

28 As soon as I have delivered this money and completed this good deed of theirs, I will come to see you on my way to Spain.

29 And I am sure that when I come the Lord will give me a great blessing for you.

30 Will you be my prayer partners? For the Lord Jesus Christ's sake, and because of your love for me—given to you by the Holy Spirit—pray much with me for my work.

31 Pray that I will be protected from those who are not Christians in Jerusalem. Pray also that the Christians there will be willing to accept the money I am bringing them.

32 Then I will be able to come to you with a happy heart by the will of God, and we can refresh each other.

33 And now may our God, Who gives peace, be with you all. Amen.

CHAPTER 16

Phoebe, a dear Christian woman from the town of Cenchrea, will be coming to see you soon. She has worked hard in the church there. Receive her as your sister in the Lord, giving her a warm Christian welcome. Help her in every way you can, for she has helped many in their needs, including me.

3 Tell Priscilla and Aquila "hello." They have been my fellow workers in the affairs of Christ Jesus.

4 In fact, they risked their lives for me; and I am not the only one who is thankful to them: so are all the Gentile churches.

5 Please give my greetings to all those who meet to worship in their home. Greet my good friend Epaenetus. He was the very first person to become a Christian in Asia.

6 Remember me to Mary, too, who has worked so hard to help us.

7 Then there are Andronicus and Junias, my relatives who were in prison with me. They are respected by the apostles, and became Christians before I did. Please give them my greetings.

8 Say "hello" to Amplias, whom I love as one of God's own children,

9 And Urbanus, our fellow worker, and beloved Stachys.

10 Then there is Apelles, a good man whom the

Lord approves, greet him for me. And give my best regards to those working at the house of Aristobulus.

11 Remember me to Herodion my relative. Remember me to the Christian slaves over at Narcissus House.

12 Say "hello" to Tryphena and Tryphosa, the Lord's workers; and to dear Persis, who has worked so hard for the Lord.

13 Greet Rufus for me, whom the Lord picked out to be His very own; and also his dear mother who has been such a mother to me.

14 And please give my greetings to Asyncritus, Phlegon, Hermes, Patrobas, Hermas, and the other brothers who are with them.

15 Give my love to Philologus, Julia, Nereus and his sister, and to Olympas, and all the Christians who are with them.

16 Shake hands warmly with each other. All the churches here send you their greetings.

17 And now there is one more thing to say before I end this letter. Stay away from those who cause divisions and scandals, teaching things about Christ that are against what you have been taught.

18 Such teachers are not working for our Lord Jesus, but only want gain for themselves. They are good speakers and simple-minded people are often fooled by them.

19 But everyone knows that you stand loyal and true. This makes me happy indeed. I want you to remain always very clear about what is right, and to stay innocent of any wrong.

20 The God of peace will soon crush Satan under

your feet. The blessings from our Lord Jesus Christ be upon you.

21 Timothy my fellow-worker, and Lucius and Jason and Sosipater, my relatives, send you their good wishes.

22 I, Tertius, the one who is writing this letter for Paul, send my greetings too, as a Christian brother.

23 Gaius says to say "hello" to you for him. I am his guest, and the church meets here in his home. Erastus, the city treasurer, sends you his greetings and so does Quartus, a Christian brother.

24 Goodbye. May the grace of our Lord Jesus Christ be with you all.

25-27 I commit you to God, Who is able to make you strong and steady in the Lord, just as the Gospel says, and just as I have told you. This is God's plan of salvation for you Gentiles, kept secret from the beginning of time. But now as the prophets foretold and as God commands, this message is being preached everywhere, so that people all around the world will have faith in Christ and obey Him. To God, Who alone is wise, be the glory forever through Jesus Christ our Lord. Amen.

Sincerely,
Paul

I Corinthians

CHAPTER 1

From: Paul, chosen by God to be Jesus Christ's missionary, and from brother Sosthenes.

2 *To:* The Christians in Corinth, invited by God to be His people and made acceptable to Him by Christ Jesus. *And to:* All Christians everywhere—whoever calls upon the Name of Jesus Christ, our Lord and theirs.

3 May God our Father and the Lord Jesus Christ give you all of His blessings, and great peace of heart and mind.

4 I can never stop thanking God for all the wonderful gifts He has given you, now that you are Christ's:

5 He has enriched your whole life. He has helped you speak out for Him and has given you a full understanding of the truth;

6 What I told you Christ could do for you has happened!

7 Now you have every grace and blessing; every spiritual gift and power for doing His will are yours during this time of waiting for our Lord Jesus Christ to return.

8 And He guarantees right up to the end that you will be counted free from all sin and guilt on that day when He returns.

9 God will surely do this for you, for He always does just what He says, and He is the One Who invited you into this wonderful friendship with His Son, even Christ our Lord.

10 But, dear brothers, I beg you in the name of the Lord Jesus Christ to stop arguing among yourselves. Let there be real harmony. I plead with you to be of one mind, all seeing things from the same point of view.

11 For some of those who live at Chloe's house told me of your arguments and quarrels, dear brothers.

12 Some of you are saying, "I am a follower of Paul"; and others say that they are for Apollos or for Peter; and some that they alone are the true followers of Christ.

13 And so, in effect, you have broken Christ into many pieces. But did I, Paul, die for your sins? Were any of you baptized in my name?

14 I am so thankful now that I didn't baptize any of you except Crispus and Gaius.

15 For now no one can think that I have been trying to start something new, beginning a "Church of Paul."

16 Oh yes, and I baptized the family of Stephanas. I don't remember ever baptizing anyone else.

17 For Christ didn't send me to baptize, but to preach the Gospel; and even my preaching sounds poor, for I do not fill my sermons with profound words and high sounding ideas, for fear of diluting the mighty power there is in the simple message of the cross of Christ.

18 I know very well how foolish it sounds to those

who are lost when they hear that Jesus died to save them. But we who are saved recognize this message as the very power of God.

19 For God says, "I will destroy all human plans of salvation no matter how wise they seem to be, and ignore the best ideas of men, even the most brilliant of them."

20 So what about these wise men, these scholars, these brilliant debaters of this world's great affairs? God has made them all look foolish, and shown their wisdom to be useless nonsense.

21 For God in His wisdom saw to it that the world would never find God through human brilliance, and then He stepped in and saved all those who believed His message, which the world calls foolish and silly.

22 It seems foolish to the Jews because they want a sign from heaven as proof that what is preached is true; and it is foolish to thc Gentiles because they only believe what agrees with their science and seems wise to them.

23 So when we preach about Christ dying to save them, the Jews are offended and the Gentiles say it's all nonsense.

24 But God has opened the eyes of those called to salvation, both Jews and Gentiles, to see that Christ is the mighty power of God to save them; Christ Himself is The Center of God's wise plan for their salvation.

25 This so-called "foolish" plan of God is far wiser than the wisest plan of the wisest man, and God in His weakness—Christ dying on the cross—is far stronger than any man.

26 Notice among ourselves, dear brothers, that few

of us who follow Christ have big names or power or wealth.

27 Instead, God has deliberately chosen to save those whom the world considers foolish and of little worth in order to shame those the world considers wise and great.

28 He has chosen the little people, those despised by the world, who just don't count for anything at all, and used them to bring down to nothing those the world considers great,

29 So that no one anywhere can ever brag in the presence of God.

30 For it is from God alone that you have your life through Christ Jesus. He showed us God's plan of salvation; He was the One Who made us acceptable to God; He made us pure and holy and gave Himself to purchase our salvation.

31 As it says in the Scriptures, "If anyone is going to boast, let him only boast of what the Lord has done."

CHAPTER 2

Dear brothers, even when I first came to you I didn't use lofty words and brilliant ideas to tell you God's message.

2 For I decided that I would speak only of Jesus Christ and His death on the cross.

3 I came to you in weakness—timid and trembling.

4 And my preaching was very plain, not with a lot of oratory and human wisdom, but God's power was in

my words, proving to those who heard them that the message was from God.

5 I did this because I wanted your faith to stand firmly upon God, not on some man's great ideas.

6 Yet when I am among mature Christians I do speak with words of great wisdom, but not the kind that comes from here on earth, and not the kind that appeals to the great men of this world, who are doomed to fall.

7 Our words are wise because they are from God, telling of God's wise plan to bring us into the glories of heaven. This plan was hidden in former times, though it was made for our benefit before the world began.

8 But the great men of the world have not understood it; if they had, they never would have crucified the Lord of Glory.

9 That is what is meant by the Scriptures which say that no mere man has ever seen, heard or even imagined what wonderful things God has ready for those who love the Lord.

10 But we know about these things because God has sent His Spirit to tell us, and His Spirit searches out and shows us all of God's deepest secrets.

11 No one can really know what anyone else is thinking, or what he is really like, except that person himself. And no one can know God's thoughts except God's own Spirit.

12 And God has actually given us His Spirit (not the world's spirit) to tell us about the wonderful free gifts of grace and blessing that God has given us.

13 In telling you about these gifts we have even

used the very words given us by the Holy Spirit, not words that we as men might choose. So we use the Holy Spirit's words to explain the Holy Spirit's facts.

14 But the man who isn't a Christian can't understand and can't accept these thoughts from God, which the Holy Spirit teaches us. They sound foolish to him, because only those who have the Holy Spirit within them can understand what the Holy Spirit means. Others just can't take it in.

15 But the spiritual man fully understands it, and that bothers and baffles the man of the world, who can't understand him at all.

16 How could he? For certainly he has never been one to know the Lord's thoughts, or to discuss them with Him, or move the hands of God by prayer. But, strange as it seems, we Christians actually do have within us a portion of the very thoughts and mind of Christ.

CHAPTER 3

Dear brothers, I have been talking to you as though you were still just babies in the Christian life, who are not following the Lord, but your own desires; I cannot talk to you as I would to healthy Christians, who are filled with the Spirit.

2 I have had to feed you with milk and not with solid food, because you couldn't digest anything stronger. And even now you still have to be fed on milk.

3 For you are still only baby Christians, controlled by your own desires, not God's. When you are jealous of one another and divide up into quarreling groups, doesn't that prove you are still babies, wanting your

own way? In fact, you are acting like people who don't belong to the Lord at all.

4 There you are, quarreling about whether I am greater than Apollos and dividing the church. Doesn't this show how little you have grown in the Lord?

5 Who am I, and who is Apollos, that we should be the cause of a quarrel? Why, we're just God's servants, each of us with certain special abilities, and with our help you believed.

6 My work was to plant the seed in your hearts, and Apollos' work was to water it, but it was God, not we, Who made the garden grow in your hearts.

7 A person who does the planting or watering isn't very important, but God is important because He is the One who makes things grow.

8 Apollos and I are working as a team, with the same aim, though each of us will be rewarded for his own hard work.

9 We are only God's co-workers. You are *God's* garden, not ours; you are *God's* building, not ours.

10 God, in His kindness, has taught me how to be an expert builder. I have laid the foundation and Apollos has built on it. But he who builds on the foundation must be very careful.

11 For no one can ever lay any other real foundation than the one we already have—Jesus Christ.

12 But there are various kinds of materials that can be used to build on that foundation. Some use gold and silver and jewels; and some build with sticks, and hay, or even straw!

13 There is going to come a time of testing at

Christ's Judgment Day to see what kind of material each builder has used. Everyone's work will be put through the fire so that all can see whether or not it keeps its value, and what was really accomplished.

14 Then every workman who has built on the Foundation with the right materials, and whose work still stands, will get his pay.

15 But if the house he has built burns up, he will have a great loss. He himself will be saved, but like a man escaping through a wall of flames.

16 Don't you realize that all of you together are the house of God, and that the Spirit of God lives among you in His house?

17 If anyone defiles and spoils God's home, God will destroy him. For God's home is holy and clean, and you are that home.

18 Stop fooling yourselves. If you count yourself above average in intelligence, as judged by this world's standards, you had better put this all aside and be a fool rather than let it hold you back from the true wisdom from above.

19 For the wisdom of this world is foolishness to God. As it says in the book of Job, God uses man's own brilliance to trap him; he stumbles over his own "wisdom" and falls.

20 And again, in the book of Psalms, we are told that the Lord knows full well how the human mind reasons, and how foolish and futile it is.

21 So don't be proud of following the wise men of this world. For God has already given you everything you need.

22 He has given you Paul and Apollos and Peter as your helpers. He has given you the whole world to use, and life and even death are your servants to bring you to Christ. He has given you all of the present and all of the future. All are yours,

23 And you belong to Christ, and Christ is God's.

CHAPTER 4

So Apollos and I should be looked upon as Christ's servants who distribute God's treasure, explaining God's secrets to others.

2 Now the most important thing about a servant is that he does just what his master tells him to.

3 What about me? Have I been a good servant? Well, I don't worry over what you think about this, or what anyone else thinks. I don't even trust my own judgment on this point.

4 My conscience is clear, but even that isn't final proof. It is the Lord Himself who must examine me and decide.

5 So be careful not to jump to conclusions before the Lord returns as to whether someone is a good servant or not. When the Lord comes, He will turn on the light so that everyone can see exactly what each one of us is really like, deep down in our hearts. Then everyone will know why we have been doing the Lord's work. At that time God will give to each one whatever praise is coming to him.

6 I have used Apollos and myself as examples to illustrate what I have been saying, that you must not

judge others. You must not be proud of one of God's teachers more than another.

7 What are you so puffed up about? What do you have that God hasn't given you? And if all you have is from God, why act as though you were so great, and as though you have accomplished something on your own?

8 You seem to think you already have all the spiritual food you need. You are full and spiritually contented, rich kings on your thrones, leaving us far behind! I wish you really were already on your thrones, for when that time comes you can be sure that we will be there, too, reigning with you.

9 Sometimes I think God has put us apostles at the very end of the line, like prisoners soon to be killed, put on display at the end of a victor's parade, to be stared at by men and angels alike.

10 Religion has made us queer, you say, but of course you are all such wise and sensible Christians! We are weak, but not you! You are well thought of, while we are laughed at.

11 To this very hour we have gone hungry and thirsty, without enough clothes to keep us warm. We have been kicked around without homes of our own.

12 We have worked wearily with our hands to earn our living. We have blessed those who cursed us. We have been patient with those who injured us.

13 We have replied quietly when evil things have been said about us. Yet right up to the present moment we are like dirt under foot, like garbage.

14 I am not writing about these things to make you

ashamed, but to warn and counsel you as beloved children.

15 For although you may have ten thousand others to teach you about Christ, remember that you have only me as your father. For I was the one who brought you to Christ when I preached the Gospel to you.

16 So I beg you to follow my example, and do as I do.

17 That is the very reason why I have sent Timothy, to help you do this. For he is one of those I won to Christ, a beloved and trustworthy child in the Lord. He will remind you of the way I do things as a Christian, which I teach in all the churches wherever I go.

18 I know that some of you have become proud, thinking that I am afraid to come to deal with you.

19 But I will come, and soon, if the Lord will let me, and then I'll find out whether these proud men are just big talkers or whether they really have God's power.

20 The kingdom of God is not just talking; it is living by God's power.

21 Which do you choose? Shall I come with punishment and scolding, or shall I come with quiet love and gentleness?

CHAPTER 5

Everyone is talking about the terrible thing that has happened there among you, something so wicked that even the heathen don't do it; and yet you have a man in your church who is living in sin with his father's wife.†

†Possibly his step-mother.

2 And are you still so conceited, so "spiritual"? Why aren't you mourning in sorrow and shame, and seeing to it that this man is removed from your membership?

3, 4 Although I am not there with you, I have been thinking a lot about this, and in the name of the Lord Jesus Christ I have already decided what to do, just as though I were there. You are to call a meeting of the church—and the power of the Lord Jesus will be with you as you meet, and I will be there in spirit—

5 And cast out this man from the fellowship of the church and into Satan's hands, to punish him, in the hope that this will wake him up and save his soul before it is too late, when our Lord Jesus Christ returns.

6 What a terrible thing it is that you are boasting about your purity, and yet you let this sort of thing go on. Don't you realize that if even one person is allowed to go on sinning, soon all will be affected?

7 Remove this evil cancer—this evil person—from among you, so that you can stay pure. Christ, God's lamb has been slain for us.

8 So let us feast upon Him and grow strong in the Christian life, leaving entirely behind us the cancerous old life with all its hatreds and wickedness. Let us feast instead upon the pure bread of honor and sincerity and truth.

9 When I wrote to you before I said not to mix with evil people.

10 But when I said that I wasn't talking about unbelievers who live in sexual sin, or are greedy cheats and thieves and idol worshipers. For you can't live in this world without being with people like that.

11 What I meant was not to keep company with anyone who claims to be a brother Christian but indulges in sexual sins, or is greedy and unfair, or is a swindler, or worships idols, or is a drunkard, or foul mouthed. Don't even eat lunch with such a person.

12 It isn't our job to judge outsiders. But it certainly is our job to judge and deal strongly with those who are members of the church, and who are sinning in these ways.

13 God alone is the Judge of those on the outside. But you yourselves must deal with this man and put him out of your church.

CHAPTER 6

How is it that when you have something against another Christian, you "go to law" and ask a heathen court to decide the matter instead of taking it to other Christians to decide which of you is right?

2 Don't you know that some day we Christians are going to judge and govern the world? So why can't you decide even these little things among yourselves?

3 Don't you realize that we Christians will judge and reward the very angels in heaven? So you should be able to decide your problems down here on earth easily enough.

4 Why then go to outside judges who are not even Christians?†

5 I am trying to make you ashamed. Isn't there

†Or, "Even the least capable people in the church should be able to decide these things for you." Both interpretations are possible.

anyone in all the church who is wise enough to decide these arguments?

6 But instead one Christian sues another and accuses his Christian brother in front of unbelievers.

7 To have such arguments at all is a real defeat for you as Christians. Why not just accept mistreatment and leave it at that? It would be far more honoring to the Lord to let yourself be cheated.

8 But instead you yourselves are the ones who do wrong, cheating others, even your own brothers.

9, 10 Don't you know that those doing such things have no share in the kingdom of God? Don't fool yourselves. Those who live immoral lives—who are idol worshipers, adulterers or homosexuals—will have no share in His kingdom. Neither will thieves and cheaters, drunkards, slandermongers, and robbers.

11 There was a time when some of you were just like that but now your sins are washed away, and you are set apart for God, and He has accepted you because of what the Lord Jesus Christ and the Spirit of our God have done for you.

12 I can do anything I want to if Christ has not said "No,"† but some of these things aren't good for me. Even if I am allowed to do them, I'll refuse to if I think that they might get such a grip on me that I can't easily stop when I want to.

13 For instance, take the matter of eating. God has given us an appetite for food and stomachs to digest it. But that doesn't mean we should eat more than we

---

†implied. Obviously, Paul is not here permitting sins such as have just been expressly prohibited in verses 8 and 9. He is talking about indifferent matters such as eating meat offered to idols. See chapter 8.

need. Don't think of eating as important, because some day God will do away with both stomachs and food. But sexual sin is never right: our bodies were not made for that, but for the Lord, and the Lord wants to fill our bodies with Himself.

14 And God is going to raise our bodies from the dead by His power just as He raised up the Lord Jesus Christ.

15 Don't you realize that your bodies are actually parts and members of Christ? So should I take part of Christ and join Him to an harlot? Never!

16 And don't you know that if a man joins himself to an harlot that she becomes a part of him and he becomes a part of her? For God tells in the Old Testament that in His sight the two become one person.

17 But if you give yourself to the Lord, you and Christ are joined together as one person.

18 That is why I say run from sex sin. Every other sinful thing a man does hurts someone else, but this is sinning against his own body.

19 Haven't you yet learned that your body is the home of the Holy Spirit God gave you, and that He lives within you? Your own body does not belong to you,

20 For God has bought you with a great price. So use every part of your body to give glory back to God, because He owns it.

CHAPTER 7

Now about those questions you asked in your last letter: my answer is that if you do not marry, it is good.

2 But usually it is best to be married, each man having his own wife, and each woman having her own husband, because otherwise you might fall back into sin.

3 The man should give his wife all that is her right as a married woman, and the wife should do the same for her husband:

4 For a girl who marries no longer has full right to her own body, for her husband then has his rights to it, too. And in the same way the husband no longer has full right to his own body, for it belongs also to his wife.

5 So do not refuse these rights to each other. The only exception to this rule would be the agreement of both husband and wife to refrain from the rights of marriage for a limited time, so that they can give themselves more completely to fasting and prayer. Afterwards they should come together again so that Satan won't be able to tempt them because of their lack of self control.

6 I'm not saying you *must* marry; but you certainly *may* if you wish.

7 I wish everyone could get along without marrying, just as I do. But we are not all the same. God gives some the gift of a husband or wife, and others He gives the gift of being able to stay happily unmarried.

8 So I say to those who aren't married, and to widows—better stay unmarried if you can, just as I am.

9 But if you can't control yourselves, go ahead and marry. It is better to marry than to burn with lust.

10 Now, for those who are married I have a command, not just a suggestion. And it is not a command from me, for this is what the Lord Himself has said: a wife must not leave her husband.

11 But if she is already separated from him, let her remain single or else go back to him again. And the husband must not leave his wife.

12 Here I want to add some suggestions of my own; these are not direct commands from the Lord, but they seem right to me. If a Christian has a wife who is not a Christian, but she wants to stay with him anyway, he must not leave her or divorce her.

13 And if a Christian woman has a husband who isn't a Christian, and he wants her to stay with him, she must not leave him.

14 For perhaps the husband who isn't a Christian may become a Christian with the help of his Christian wife. And the wife who isn't a Christian may become a Christian with the help of her Christian husband. Otherwise, if the family separates, the children might never come to know the Lord. But for a family to stay together may, in God's plan, result in the children's salvation.

15 But if the husband or wife who isn't a Christian is eager to leave, let him go. The Christian husband or wife should not insist that the other stay in such cases, for God wants His children to live in peace and harmony.

16 For after all, there is no assurance to you wives that your husbands will be saved if they stay; and the same may be said to you husbands concerning your wives.

17 But be sure in deciding these matters that you are living as God intended, marrying or not marrying in accordance with God's direction and help, and accepting whatever situation God has put you into. This is my rule for all the churches.

18 For instance, a man who already has gone

through the Jewish ceremony of circumcision before he became a Christian shouldn't worry about it; and if he hasn't been circumcised, he shouldn't do it now.

19 For it doesn't make any difference at all whether a Christian has gone through this ceremony or not. But it makes a lot of difference whether he is pleasing God and keeping God's commandments. That is the important thing.

20 Usually a person should keep on with the work he was doing when God called him.

21 Are you a slave? Don't let that worry you,—but of course if you get a chance to be free, take it.

22 If the Lord calls you, and you are a slave, remember that Christ has set you free from the awful power of sin; and if He has called you and you are free, remember that you are now a slave of Christ.

23 You have been bought and paid for by Christ, so you belong to Him now, not just to earthly masters.

24 So, dear brothers, in whatever situation a person is when he becomes a Christian, let him stay there, for now the Lord is there to help him.

25 Now I will try to answer your other question. What about girls who are not yet married? Should they be permitted to marry? I have no special command for them from the Lord. But the Lord in His kindness has given me wisdom that can be trusted, and I will be glad to tell you what I think.

26 Here is the problem: we Christians are facing great dangers to our lives at present. In times like these I think it is best for a person not to be married.

27 Of course if you already are, don't separate be-

cause of this. But if you aren't married, don't rush into marriage at this time.

28 But if you men decide to go ahead anyway and get married now, it is all right; and if a maiden marries now, it is no sin. However, marriage will bring extra problems that I wish you didn't have to face right now.

29 The important thing to remember is that our remaining time is very short, and so are our opportunities for doing the Lord's work. For that reason those who have wives should stay as free as possible for the Lord;

30 Happiness or sadness or wealth should not keep anyone from doing God's work;

31 Those in frequent contact with the exciting things the world offers should make good use of their opportunities without stopping to enjoy them; for the world in its present form will soon be gone.

32 In all you do, I want you to be free from worry. An unmarried man can spend his time doing the Lord's work and thinking how to please Him.

33 But a married man can't do that so well; he has to think about his responsibilities down here on earth and how to please his wife.

34 His interests are divided. It is the same with a girl who marries. She faces the same problem. A girl who is not married is anxious to please the Lord in all she is and does. But a married woman must consider other things such as housekeeping and the likes and dislikes of her husband.

35 I am saying this to help you, not to try to keep you from marrying. I want you to do whatever will

help you serve the Lord best, with as few other things as possible to distract your attention from Him.

36 But if anyone feels he ought to marry because he is being unfair to the one he loves, and she is getting older and wants to marry, it is all right, it is not a sin; let them marry.

37 But if a man has the will power not to marry and decides that he doesn't need to and won't, he has made a wise decision.

38 So the person who marries does well, and the person who doesn't marry does even better.

39 The wife is part of her husband as long as he lives; if her husband dies, then she may marry again, but only if she marries a Christian.

40 But she probably will be happier if she doesn't marry again; and I think I am giving you counsel from God's Spirit when I say this.

CHAPTER 8

Next is your question about eating food that has been sacrificed to idols. On this question everyone feels that only his answer is the right one! But although being a "know-it-all" makes us feel important, what we really need to build the church is love.

2 If anyone thinks he knows all the answers, he's just showing his ignorance.

3 But the person who truly loves God is the one who is God's friend.

4 So now, what about it? Should we eat meat that has been sacrificed to idols? Well, we all know that an

idol is not really a god, and that there is only one God, and no other.

5 There are of course many things that people think are gods, and call gods and lords, both in the sky and down here on earth.

6 But we know that there is only one God, the Father, Who created all things and made us to be His own; and one Lord Jesus Christ, Who made everything and gives us life.

7 But some Christians don't realize this; all their lives they have been used to thinking of idols as alive, and that the food offered to the idols was being offered to actual gods. So when they eat such food it bothers them and hurts their tender consciences.

8 Just remember that God doesn't care whether we eat it or not. We are no worse off if we don't eat it, and no better off if we do.

9 But watch out, if you use your freedom to eat it, lest you hurt some Christian brother whose faith is weaker than yours.

10 You see, this is what may happen: someone who thinks it is wrong to eat this food will see you eating at a temple restaurant, for you know there is no harm in it. Then he will become bold enough to do it too. But all the time he will still feel it is wrong.

11 So you will be responsible for causing great spiritual damage to a brother with a tender conscience, for whom Christ died. For he will be doing what he thinks is wrong.

12 And it is a sin against Christ to sin against your

brother by encouraging him to do something he thinks is wrong.

13 So if eating meat offered to idols is going to make my brother sin, I'll not eat any of it as long as I live, because I don't want to hurt him in any way.

CHAPTER 9

I am an apostle, God's messenger, responsible to no mere man. I am one who has actually seen Jesus our Lord with my own eyes. And your changed lives are the result of my hard work for God.

2 If I am not an apostle in the opinion of others, I certainly am to you, for you have been won to Christ through me.

3 That is my answer to those who question my rights.

4 Or don't I have any rights at all? Can't I claim the same privilege the other apostles do of being a guest in your homes?

5 If I had a Christian wife, couldn't I bring her along on these trips just as the other disciples do, and as the Lord's brothers, do, and as Peter does?

6 Must Barnabas and I alone keep working for our living, while you supply these others?

7 What soldier in the army has to pay his own expenses? And have you ever heard of a farmer who harvests his crop and doesn't have the right to eat some of it? What shepherd takes care of a flock of sheep and cows and isn't allowed to drink some of the milk?

8 And I'm not merely quoting the opinions of men

as to what is right. I'm telling you what God's law says.

9 For in the law God gave to Moses He said that you must not put a muzzle on an ox to keep it from eating when it is treading out the corn. Do you think God was thinking only about oxen when He said this?

10 Wasn't He also thinking about us? Of course He was. He said this to show us that Christian workers should be paid by those they help. Those who do the plowing and threshing should expect some share of the harvest.

11 We have planted good spiritual seed in your souls. Is it too much to ask, in return, for mere food and clothing and other needs for our bodies?

12 Others who preach to you get these gifts from you, and they should. But shouldn't we have an even greater right to them? Yet we have *never* used this right; we have never demanded payment of any kind for fear that, if we did, you might be less interested in the message from Christ which we have for you.

13 Don't you realize that God told those working in His temple to take for their own needs some of the food brought there as gifts to Him? And those who work at the altar of God get a share of the food that is brought by those offering it to the Lord.

14 In the same way the Lord has given orders that those who preach the Gospel should be paid by those who accept it.

15 Yet I have never asked you for one penny. And I am not writing this to hint that I would like to start now. In fact I would rather die of hunger than lose this glorious privilege of preaching to you without charge.

16 For just preaching the Gospel isn't any special credit to me—I couldn't keep from preaching it if I wanted to. I would be utterly miserable. Woe unto me if I don't.

17 If I were volunteering my services of my own free will, then the Lord would give me a special reward; but that is not the situation, for God has picked me out and given me this sacred trust and I have no choice.

18 Under this circumstance, what is my pay? It is the special joy I get from preaching the Good News without expense to anyone, never demanding my rights.

19 And this has a real advantage: I am not bound to obey anyone just because he pays my salary; yet I have freely and happily become a servant of any and all so that I can win them to Christ.

20 When I am with the Jews I seem as one of them so that they will listen to the Gospel and I can win them to Christ. When I am with Gentiles who follow Jewish customs and ceremonies I don't argue, even though I don't agree, because I want to help them.

21 When with the heathen I agree with them as much as I can, except of course that I must always do what is right as a Christian. And so, by agreeing, I can win their confidence and help them too.

22 When I am with those whose consciences bother them easily. I don't act as though I know it all and say they are being foolish; so they, too, will let me help them. Yes, whatever a person is like, I try to find common ground with him so that he will be willing to let me tell him of Christ.

23 I do this to get the Gospel to them and also for

the blessing I myself receive when I see them come to Christ.

24 In a race everyone runs but only one person gets first prize. So run your race to win.

25 To win the contest you must deny yourselves many things that would keep you from doing your best. An athlete goes to all this trouble just to win a blue ribbon or a silver cup,† but we do it for a heavenly reward that never disappears.

26 So I run straight to the goal with purpose in every step. I fight to win. I'm not just shadow-boxing or playing around.

27 Like an athlete I punish my body, treating it roughly, training it to do what it should, not what it wants to. Otherwise I fear that after enlisting others for the race, I myself might be declared unfit and ordered to stand aside.

CHAPTER 10

For we must never forget, dear brothers, what happened to our people in the wilderness long ago. God made them safe and guided them by sending a cloud that moved along ahead of them; and He brought them all safely through the waters of the Red Sea.

2 This might be called their baptism both in the water and the cloud, as followers of Moses—their commitment to him as their leader.

3, 4 And by a miracle God sent them food to eat and water to drink there in the desert; they drank the

† literally: "a wreath that quickly fades" given to the winners of the original Olympic races of Paul's time.

water that Christ gave them. He was there with them as a mighty Rock of spiritual refreshment.

5 Yet after all this most of them did not please God, and He destroyed them in the wilderness.

6 From this we learn a terrible lesson: that we must not desire evil things as they did,

7 Nor worship idols as they did. (The Scriptures tell us "The people sat down to eat and drink and then got up to dance" in worship of the golden calf.)

8 Another lesson for us is what happened when some of them sinned with other men's wives, and 23,000 fell dead in one day.

9 And don't try the Lord's patience as they did—and died from snake bites.

10 And don't murmur against God and His dealings with you as some of them did; for that is why God sent his Angel to destroy them.

11 All these things happened to them as examples, as object lessons to us, to warn us against doing the same things; they were written down so that we could read about them and learn from them in these last days as the world nears its end.

12 So be careful. If you are thinking, "Oh, I would never behave like that"—let this be a warning to you. For you too may fall into sin.

13 But remember this, the wrong desires that come into your life aren't new and different. Many others have faced exactly the same problems before you. And you can trust God to keep temptation from becoming so strong that you can't stand up against it, for He has promised this and will do what He says. He will show

you how to escape temptation's power so that you can bear up patiently against it.

14 So, dear friends, carefully avoid idol-worship of every kind.

15 You are intelligent people. Look now and see for yourselves whether what I am about to say is true.

16 When we ask the Lord's blessing upon our drinking from the cup of wine at the Lord's Table, this means, doesn't it, that all who drink it are sharing together the blessing of Christ's blood? And the bread we eat there shows that we are sharing together in the benefits of His body that was broken for us.

17 No matter how many of us there are, we all eat from the same loaf, showing we are all parts of the one body of Christ.

18 And the Jewish priests, when they ate of the animals brought to God as sacrifices, were showing that they were partners with God.

19 What am I trying to say? Am I saying that the idols to whom the heathen bring sacrifices are really alive and are real gods, and that these sacrifices are of some value? No, not at all.

20 What I am saying is that those who offer food to idols are really sacrificing to demons, certainly not to God. And I don't want any of you to be partners with demons when you eat the same food, along with the heathen, that has been offered to these idols.

21 You cannot drink from the cup at the Lord's Table and at Satan's table, too. You cannot eat bread both at the Lord's Table and at Satan's table.

22 What? Are you tempting the Lord to be angry with you? Are you stronger than He is?

23 You are certainly free to eat food offered to idols if you want to; it's not against God's laws to eat such meat, but that doesn't mean that you should go ahead and do it. It may be perfectly legal, but it may not be best and helpful.

24 Don't think only of yourself. Try to think of the other fellow, too, and what is best for him.

25 Here's what you should do. Take any meat you want that is sold at the market. Don't ask whether or not it was offered to idols for fear the answer will hurt your conscience.

26 For the earth and every good thing in it belongs to the Lord and is yours to enjoy.

27 If someone who isn't a Christian asks you out to dinner, go ahead, accept the invitation if you want to, and eat whatever is on the table but don't ask any questions about it. Then you won't know and won't risk having a bad conscience over it.

28 But if someone warns you that this meat has been offered to idols, then don't eat it for the sake of the man who told you and his conscience.

29 In this case *his* feeling about it is the important thing, not yours. But why, you may ask, must I be guided and limited by what someone else thinks?

30 If I can thank God for the food and enjoy it, why let someone spoil everything just because he thinks I am wrong?

31 Well, I'll tell you why. It is because you must

do everything for the glory of God, even your eating and drinking.

32 So don't be a stumblingblock to anyone, whether they are Jews or Gentiles or Christians.

33 That is the plan I follow, too. I try to please everyone in everything I do, not doing what I like or what is best for me, but what is best for them, so that they may be saved.

CHAPTER 11

And you should follow my example, just as I follow Christ's.

2 I am so glad, dear brothers, that you have been remembering and doing all I taught you.

3 But there is one matter I want to remind you about: that a wife is responsible to her husband; her husband is responsible to Christ; and Christ is responsible to God.

4 That is why, if a man prays or preaches with his hat on, (showing subjection to man instead of to Christ)† he dishonors Christ.

5 And that is why a woman who publicly prays or prophesies without a covering on her head dishonors her husband (for her covering is a sign of her subjection to man, and having her head uncovered is a sign of rebellion against him).†

6 Yes, if she refuses to wear a head covering, then she should cut off all her hair. And if it is shameful for

† Implied.

a woman to have her head shaved, then she should wear a covering.

7 But a man should *not* wear anything on his head (in church, for a hat is a sign of subjection to man, not Christ).† The man is the image and glory of God; and the man's glory is the woman.

8 The first man didn't come from woman, but the first woman came out of man. (See Genesis 2:21-22).

9 And Adam, the first man, was not made for Eve's benefit, but Eve was made for Adam.

10 So a woman should wear a covering on her head as a sign that she is under man's authority,† for all the angels to see and rejoice in.

11 But remember that in God's plan men and women need each other.

12 For although the first woman came out of man, all men have been born from women ever since, and both men and women come from God their Creator.

13 What do you yourselves really think about this? Is it right for a woman to pray in public without covering her head?

14, 15 Doesn't even nature itself teach us that women's heads should be covered? For nature gives long hair to women—and they are proud of it—while men have short hair and are ashamed when it gets long.

16 But if anyone wants to argue about this, all I can say is that we never teach anything else than this—that a woman should wear a covering when prophesying or praying publicly in the church, and all the churches feel the same way about it.

17 Next on my list of items to write you about is

† literally: "For this cause ought the woman to have power on (her) head."

something else I cannot agree with. For it sounds as if more harm is done than good when you meet together for your communion services.

18 Everyone keeps telling me about the arguing that goes on in these meetings, and the divisions developing among you, and I can just about believe it.

19 But I suppose you feel this is necessary so that you who are always right will become known and recognized!

20 When you come together to eat, it isn't the Lord's Supper you are eating,

21 But your own. For I am told that everyone hastily gobbles all the food he can get hold of without waiting to share with each other, so that one doesn't get enough and goes hungry while another has too much to drink and gets drunk.

22 What? Is this really true? Can't you eat and drink at home without disgracing the church and shaming those who are poor and can bring no food? What am I supposed to say about these things? Do you want me to praise you? Well, I certainly do not!

23 For this is what the Lord Himself has said about His Table, and I have passed it on to you before: That on the night when Judas betrayed Him, the Lord Jesus took bread,

24 And when He had given thanks to God for it, He broke it and gave it to His disciples and said "Take this and eat it. This is my body, which is broken for you. Do this to remember me."

25 In the same way, He took the cup of wine after supper, saying, "This cup is the new agreement between

God and you that has been established and set in motion by my blood. Think of this in remembrance of me whenever you drink it."

26 For every time you eat this bread and drink this cup you are re-telling the message of the Lord's death, that He has died for you. Do this until He comes again.

27 So if anyone eats this bread and drinks from this cup of the Lord when he shouldn't, he is guilty of sin against the body and the blood of the Lord.

28 That is why a man should examine himself carefully before eating the bread and drinking from the cup.

29 For if he eats the bread and drinks from the cup unworthily, not thinking about the body of Christ and what it means, he is eating and drinking God's judgment upon himself; for he is trifling with the death of Christ.

30 That is why many of you are weak and sick, and some have even died.

31 But if you carefully examine yourselves before eating you will not need to be judged and punished.

32 Yet, when we are judged and punished by the Lord, it is so that we will not be condemned with the rest of the world.

33 So, dear brothers, when you gather for the Lord's Supper—the communion service—wait for each other;

34 If anyone is really hungry he should eat first at home so that he won't bring punishment upon himself when you meet together.

I'll talk to you about the other matters after I arrive.

CHAPTER 12

And now, brothers, I want to write about the special abilities the Holy Spirit gives to each of you, for I don't want any misunderstanding about them.

2 You will remember that before you became Christians you went around from one idol to another, not one of which could speak a single word.

3 But now you are meeting people who claim to speak messages from the Spirit of God. How can you know whether they are really inspired by God or whether they are fakes? Here is the test: no one speaking by the power of the Spirit of God can curse Jesus, and no one can say "Jesus is Lord," and really mean it, unless the Holy Spirit is helping him.

4 Now God gives us many kinds of special abilities, but it is the same Holy Spirit who is the source of them all.

5 There are different kinds of service to God, but it is the same Lord we are serving.

6 There are many ways of doing His work, but it is the same God who does the work in and through all of us who are His.

7 The Holy Spirit displays God's power through each of us as a means of helping the entire church.

8 To one person the Spirit gives the ability to give wise advice; someone else may be especially good at studying, and this is his gift from the same Spirit.

9 He gives special faith to another, and to someone else the power to cure the sick.

10 He gives power for doing miracles to some; and

power to prophesy and preach to others. He gives someone else the power to know whether evil spirits are speaking through those who claim to be giving God's messages—or whether it is really the Spirit of God Who is speaking. Still another person is able to speak in languages he never learned; and others, who do not know the language either, are given power to understand what he is saying.

11 It is the same and only Holy Spirit who gives all these gifts and powers, deciding which each one of us should have.

12 Our bodies have many parts, but the many parts make only one body when they are all put together. So it is with the "body" of Christ.

13 Each of us is a part of the one body of Christ. Some of us are Jews, some are Gentiles, some are slaves and some are free. But the Holy Spirit has fitted us all together into one body. We are baptized into Christ's body by the one Spirit, and are all filled with that same Holy Spirit.

14 Yes, the body has many parts, not just one part.

15 If the foot says, "I am not a part of the body because I am not a hand," that does not make it any less a part of the body.

16 And what would you think if you heard an ear say, "I am not part of the body because I am only an ear, and not an eye?" Would that make it any less a part of the body?

17 Suppose the whole body were an eye—then how

would you hear? Or if your whole body were just one big ear, how could you smell anything?

18 But that isn't the way God has made us. He has made many parts for our bodies and has put each part just where He wants it.

19 What a strange thing a body would be if it had only one part!

20 So He has made many parts, but still there is only one body.

21 The eye can never say to the hand, "I don't need you." The head can't say to the feet, "I don't need you."

22 And some of the parts that seem weakest and least important are really the most necessary.

23 Yes, we are especially glad to have some parts that seem rather odd! And we carefully protect from the eyes of others those parts that should not be seen,

24 While of course the parts that may be seen do not require this special care. So God has put the body together in such a way that extra honor and care are given to those parts that might otherwise seem less important.

25 This makes for happiness among the parts, so that the parts have the same care for each other that they do for themselves.

26 If one part suffers, all the parts suffer with it, and if one part is honored, all the parts are glad.

27 Now here is what I am trying to say: all of you together are the one body of Christ and each one of you is a separate and necessary part of it.

28 Here is a list of some of the parts He has placed in His church, which is His body:

Apostles,
Prophets—those who preach God's word,
Teachers,
Those who do miracles,
Those who have the gift of healing,
Those who can help others,
Those who can get others to work together,
Those who speak in languages they have never learned.

29 Is everyone an apostle? Of course not. Is everyone a preacher? No. Are all teachers? Does everyone have the power of doing miracles?

30 Can everyone heal the sick? Of course not. Does God give all of us the power to speak in languages we've never learned? Can just anyone understand what those are saying who have that gift of foreign speech?

31 No, but try your best to get the greatest and best of these gifts. But first let me tell you about something else that is better than any of them!

CHAPTER 13

If I had the gift of being able to speak in other languages without learning them, and could speak in every language there is in all of heaven and earth, but didn't love others, I would only be making noise.

2 If I had the gift of prophecy and knew all about what is going to happen in the future, knew everything about *everything,* but didn't love others, what good would it do? Even if I had the gift of faith so

that I could speak to a mountain and make it move, I would still be worth nothing at all without love.

3 If I gave everything I have to poor people, and if I were burned alive for preaching the Gospel but didn't love others, it would be of no value whatever.

4 Love is very patient and kind, never jealous or envious, never boastful nor proud,

5 Never haughty nor selfish nor rude. Love does not demand its own way. It is not irritable or touchy. It does not hold grudges and will hardly even notice when others do it wrong.

6 It is never glad about injustice, but rejoices whenever truth wins out.

7 If you love someone you will be loyal to him no matter what the cost. You will always believe in him, always expect the best of him, and always stand your ground in defending him.

8 All the special gifts and powers from God will someday come to an end, but love goes on forever. Someday prophecy and speaking in unknown languages and special knowledge all will disappear.

9 For now we know so little, even with our special gifts, and the preaching of those most gifted is still so poor.

10 But when we have been made perfect and complete, then the need for these inadequate special gifts will come to an end, and they will disappear.

11 It's like this: when I was a child I spoke and thought and reasoned as a child does. But when I became a man my thoughts grew far beyond those of my childhood, and now I have put away the childish things.

12 In the same way, we can see and understand only a little about God now, as if we were peering at His reflection in a poor mirror; but someday we are going to see Him in His completeness, face to face. Now all that I know is hazy and blurred, but then I will see everything clearly, just as clearly as God sees into my heart right now.

13 There are three things—faith, hope and love—that keep on forever; but the greatest of these is love.

CHAPTER 14

Let love be your greatest aim; nevertheless, ask for the special abilities the Holy Spirit gives, and especially the gift of prophecy, being able to preach the messages of God.

2 But if your gift is that of being able to "speak in tongues," that is, to speak in languages you haven't learned, you will be talking to God but not to others, since they won't be able to understand you. You will be speaking by the power of the Spirit but it will all be a secret.

3 But one who prophesies, preaching the messages of God, is helping others grow in the Lord, encouraging and comforting them.

4 So a person "speaking in tongues" helps himself grow spiritually, but one who prophesies, preaching messages from God, helps the entire church grow in holiness and happiness.

5 I wish you all had the gift of "speaking in tongues" but, even more, I wish you were all able to prophesy, preaching God's messages, for that is a

greater and more useful power than to speak in unknown languages; unless, of course, you can tell everyone afterwards what you were saying, so that they can get some good out of it.

6 Dear friends, even if I myself should come to you talking in some language you don't understand, how would that help you? But if I speak plainly what God has revealed to me, and tell you the things I know, and what is going to happen, and the great truths of God's word, that is what you need; that is what will help you.

7 Even musical instruments—the flute, for instance, or the harp—are examples of the need for speaking in good plain English† rather than in unknown languages. For no one will recognize the tune the flute is playing unless each note is sounded clearly.

8 And if the army bugler doesn't play the right notes, how will the soldiers know what he is telling them to do? How will they know that the battle is about to begin?

9 In the same way if you talk to a person in some language he doesn't understand, how will he know what you want him to do? You might as well be talking to an empty room.

10 I suppose that there are hundreds of different languages in the world, and all are excellent for those who understand them.

11 But to me they are foreign languages. A person talking to me in one of these languages will be a stranger to me and I will be a stranger to him.

12 Since you are so anxious to have special gifts

† the local language, whatever it is.

from the Holy Spirit, ask Him for the very best, for those that will be of real help to the whole church.

13 If someone is given the gift of speaking in unknown tongues, he should pray also for the gift of knowing what he has said, so that he can tell people afterwards, plainly.

14 For if I pray in a language I don't understand, my spirit is praying but I don't know what I am saying.

15 Well then what shall I do? I will do both. I will pray in unknown tongues and also in ordinary language everybody understands. I will sing in unknown tongues and also in ordinary language, so that I can understand the praise I am giving;

16 For if you praise and thank God with the spirit alone, speaking in another language, how can those who don't understand you be praising God along with you? How can they join you in giving thanks when they don't know what you are saying?

17 You will be giving thanks very nicely, no doubt, but the other people present won't be helped.

18 I thank God that I "speak in tongues" privately† more than any of the rest of you.

19 But in public worship I would much rather speak five words that people can understand and be helped by, than ten thousand words while "speaking in tongues" in an unknown language.

20 Dear brothers, don't be childish in your understanding of these things. Be innocent babies when it comes to planning evil, but be men of intelligence in understanding matters of this kind.

† implied. See verses 19 and 28.

21 We are told in the ancient Scriptures that God would send men from other lands to speak in other languages to His people, but even so they would not listen.

22 So you see that being able to "speak in tongues" is not a help to God's children, but is to interest the unsaved. However, prophecy (preaching the deep truths of God) is what the Christians need, and unbelievers aren't yet ready for it.

23 Even so, if an unsaved person, or someone who doesn't know about these gifts, comes to church and hears you all talking in other languages, he is likely to think you are crazy.

24 But if you all prophesy, preaching God's Word, (even though such preaching is mostly for believers†) and an unsaved person or a new Christian comes in who does not understand about these things, all these sermons will convince him of the fact that he is a sinner, and his conscience will be pricked by everything he hears.

25 As he listens, his secret thoughts will be laid bare and he will fall down on his knees and worship God, knowing that God is really there among you.

26 Well, my brothers, let's add up what I am saying. When you meet together some will sing, others will teach or tell some special information God has given him, or speak in an unknown language, or tell what someone else is saying who is speaking in the unknown language, but everything that is done must be useful to all, and build them up in the Lord.

27 No more than two or three should speak in an

† implied.

unknown language, and they must speak one at a time, and someone must be ready to explain what they are saying.

28 But if no one is present who understands what they are saying, they must not speak out loud. They may talk silently to themselves and to God in the unknown language but not publicly.

29, 30 Two or three may prophesy, one at a time, if they have the gift, while all the others listen. But if, while someone is prophesying, someone else receives a message or idea from the Lord he must not interrupt, for one person should stop before another begins to speak.

31 In this way all who have the gift of prophecy can speak, one after the other, and everyone will learn and be encouraged and helped.

32 Remember that a person who has a message from God has the power to stop himself and wait his turn.

33 God is not One who likes things to be disorderly and upset. He likes harmony, and He finds it in all the other churches.

34 Women should be silent during the church meetings. They are not to take part in the discussion. They are to obey and not to teach,† as the Scriptures also command.

35 If they have any questions to ask, let them ask their husbands at home, for it is wrong for women to express their opinions in church meetings.

36 You disagree? And do you think that the knowl-

†literally: "They are not authorized to speak." They were permitted to pray and prophesy (I Cor. 11:5), apparently in public meetings, but not to teach men (I Tim. 2:12).

edge of God's will begins and ends with you Corinthians? Well, you are mistaken!

37 You who claim to have the gift of prophecy or any other special ability from the Holy Spirit should be the first to realize that what I am saying is a commandment from God Himself.

38 But if anyone still disagrees—well, we will leave him in his ignorance.

39 So, my fellow-believers, long to be prophets so that you can preach God's message plainly; and never say it is wrong to "speak in tongues;"

40 However be sure that everything is done properly in a good and orderly way.

CHAPTER 15

Now let me remind you, brothers, of what the Gospel really is, for it has not changed—it is the same Good News I preached to you before. You welcomed it and still do, for your faith is squarely built upon this wonderful message;

2 And it is this Good News that saves you if you still firmly believe it, unless of course you never really believed it in the first place.

3 I passed on to you right from the first what had been told to me, that Christ died for our sins just as the Scriptures said He would,

4 And that He was buried, and that on the third day afterwards He arose from the grave again just as the Bible foretold.

5 He was seen by Peter and later on by the rest of "The Twelve."†

6 After that he was seen by more than five hundred brethren at one time, most of whom are still alive though some are dead.

7 Then James saw Him and later all the apostles.

8 Last of all I saw Him too, long after the others, as though I had been born almost too late for this.

9 For I am the least worthy of all the apostles, and I shouldn't even be called an apostle at all after the way I treated the church of God.

10 But whatever I am now it is all because God poured out such kindness and grace upon me—and not without results: for I have worked harder than all the other apostles, yet actually I wasn't doing it, but God worked through me, helping and blessing me.

11 It makes no difference who worked the hardest, I or they; the important thing is that we preached the Gospel to you, and you believed it.

12 But tell me this! Since you believe what we preach, that *Christ* rose from the dead, why are some of you saying that there is no such thing as a resurrection day coming when *all* will come back to life again?

13 For if there is no resurrection of the dead, then Christ must still be dead.

14 And if He is still dead, then all our preaching is useless and your trust in God is empty, worthless, hopeless;

15 And we apostles are all liars because we have

---

†The name given to Jesus' twelve disciples, and still used after Judas was gone from among them.

said that God raised Christ from the grave, and of course that isn't true if the dead do not come back to life again.

16 If they don't, then Christ is still dead,

17 And you are very foolish to keep on trusting God to save you, and you are still under condemnation for your sins;

18 In that case all Christians who have died are lost!

19 And if being a Christian is only of value to us now in this life, we are the most miserable of creatures.

20 But the fact is that Christ did actually rise from the dead, and has become the first of millions now dead who will come back to life again some day.

21 Death came into the world because of what one man (Adam) did, and it is because of what this other man (Christ) has done that now there is the resurrection from the dead.

22 Everyone dies because all of us are related to Adam, being members of his sinful race, and wherever there is sin, death results. But all who are related to Christ will rise again.

23 Each, however, in his own turn: Christ rose first; then when Christ comes back, all His people will become alive again.

24 After that the end will come when He will turn the kingdom over to God the Father, having put down all enemies of every kind.

25 For Christ will be King until He has destroyed all His enemies.

26 Including the last enemy—death. This too must be destroyed and ended.

27 For the rule and authority over all things has been given to Christ by His Father; except of course Christ does not rule over the Father Himself, Who gave Him this power.

28 When Christ has finally won the battle against all His enemies, then He, the Son of God, will put Himself also under His Father's orders, so that God Who has given Him the victory over everything else will be utterly supreme.

29 If the dead will not come back to life again, then what point is there in people baptizing themselves for those who are gone? Why do it unless they believe that the dead will some day rise again?

30 And why should we ourselves be continually risking our lives, facing death hour by hour?

31 For it is a fact that I face death daily; that is as true as my joy in your growth in the Lord.

32 And what value is there in fighting wild beasts, those men of Ephesus, if it is only for what I gain in this life down here? If we will never live again after we die, then we might as well go and have ourselves a good time: let us eat, drink, and be merry. What's the difference? For tomorrow we die, and that ends everything!

33 Don't be fooled by those who say such things. If you listen to them you will start acting like them.

34 Wake up from your drunken dreams and return to your right minds and stop sinning. For to your shame I say it, some of you are not even Christians at all and have never really known God.

35 But someone may ask, "How are the dead

brought back to life again? What kind of bodies will they have?"

36 Don't ask such foolish questions! You will find the answer in your own garden! When you put a seed into the ground it doesn't grow into a plant unless it "dies" first.

37 And when the green shoot comes up out of the seed, it is very different from the seed you first planted. For all you put into the ground is a dry little seed of wheat, or whatever it is you are planting,

38 Then God gives it a beautiful new body—just the kind He wants it to have; a different kind of plant grows from each kind of seed.

39 And just as there are different kinds of seeds and plants, so also there are different kinds of flesh. Humans, animals, fish, and birds are all different.

40 The angels in heaven have bodies far different from ours. And the beauty and the glory of their bodies is different from the beauty and the glory of ours.

41 The sun has one kind of glory while the moon and stars have another kind. And the stars differ from each other in their beauty and brightness.

42 In the same way our earthly bodies which die and decay are different from the bodies we shall have when we come back to life again for they will never die.

43 The bodies we have now embarrass us for they become sick and die; but they will be full of glory when we come back to life again. Yes, they are weak, dying bodies now, but when we live again they will be full of strength.

44 They are just human bodies at death, but when

they come back to life they will be superhuman bodies. For just as there are natural, human bodies, there are also supernatural, spiritual bodies.

45 The Scriptures tell us that the first man, Adam, was given a natural human body but Christ was far more than that, for He was life-giving Spirit.

46 First we have these human bodies and later on God gives us spiritual, heavenly bodies.

47 Adam was made from the dust of the earth, but Christ came from heaven above.

48 Every human being has a body just like Adam's, made of dust, but all who become Christ's will have the same kind of body as His—a body from heaven.

49 Just as each of us now has a body like Adam's, so we shall some day have a body like Christ's.

50 I tell you this, my brothers: an earthly body made of flesh and blood cannot get into God's kingdom. These perishable bodies of ours are not the right kind to live forever.

51 But I am telling you this strange and wonderful secret: we shall not all die, but we shall all be given new bodies!

52 It will all happen in a moment, in the twinkling of an eye, when the last trumpet calls. For there will be a trumpet call from the sky and all the Christians who have died will suddenly become alive with new bodies that will never, never die; and then we who are still alive shall suddenly have new bodies, too.

53 For our earthly bodies, the ones we have now that can die, must be exchanged for our heavenly bodies that cannot perish but will live forever.

54 When this happens, then at last this Scripture will come true—"Death is swallowed up in victory."

55, 56 O death, what then of your victory? Where now your sting? You can never hurt us again, for our sin, which gives you your power over us, will all be gone; and the law, which reveals our sins, is no longer upon us.

57 How we thank God for all of this. It is He Who has made us victorious through Jesus Christ our Lord.

58 So my dear brothers, since future victory is sure, be strong and steady, always doing the Lord's work, for you know that nothing you do for the Lord is ever wasted as it would be if there were no resurrection.

CHAPTER 16

Now here are the directions about the money you are collecting to send to the Christians in Jerusalem; (and, by the way, these are the same directions I gave to the churches in Galatia).

2 Every Sunday each of you should put aside something from what you have earned during the week, and keep it for this offering. How much depends on how much the Lord has helped you earn. Don't wait until I get there and then try to collect it all at once.

3 When I come I will send your loving gift with a letter to Jerusalem, to be taken there by trustworthy messengers you yourselves will choose.

4 And if it seems wise for me to go along too, then we can travel together.

5 I am coming to visit you after I have been to

Macedonia first, but I will be staying there only for a little while.

6 It could be that I will stay longer with you, perhaps all winter, and then you can send me on again to my next destination.

7 I am not coming to see you now when I have to go right on; I don't want to come until I can stay a while, if the Lord will let me.

8 I will be staying here at Ephesus until the feast at Pentecost,

9 For there is a wide open door for me to preach and teach here. So much is happening, but there are many enemies.

10 If Timothy comes make him feel at home, for he is doing the Lord's work just as I am.

11 Don't let anyone despise or ignore him because he is young, but send him back to me happy because of his time among you, for I am looking forward to seeing him soon, as well as the others who are coming.

12 I tried to get Apollos to go over there to see you when the others came, but he didn't think it was God's time. He will be seeing you later on when he has the opportunity.

13 Keep your eyes open for spiritual danger; stand true to the Lord; act like men; be strong;

14 And whatever you do, do it with kindness and love.

15 Do you remember Stephanas and his family? They were the first to become Christians in Greece and they are spending their lives helping and serving Christians everywhere.

16 Please listen to them and do everything you can to help them and all others like them who work hard at your side with real devotion.

17 I am so glad that Stephanas, Fortunatus and Achaicus have arrived here for a visit. They have been making up for the help you aren't here to give me.

18 They have cheered me up and greatly encouraged me; I am sure they must have done the same for you. I hope you properly appreciate the work of these good men.

19 The churches here in Asia send you their loving greetings. Aquila and Priscilla send you their love and so do all the others who meet in their home for their church service.

20 All the friends here have asked me to say "hello" to you for them. And give each other a loving handshake when you meet.

21 I will write these final words of this letter with my own hand:

22 If anyone does not love the Lord, that person is cursed, for the Lord is coming soon.

23 May God's love and favor rest upon you;

24 My love to all of you, in the name of Christ Jesus. Goodby.

Sincerely,
Paul

II Corinthians

CHAPTER 1

Dear Friends,
This letter is from me, Paul, appointed by God to be Jesus Christ's messenger; and from our dear brother Timothy. We are writing to all of you Christians there in Corinth and throughout Greece.

2 May God our Father and the Lord Jesus Christ mightily bless each one of you, and give you peace.

3 What a wonderful God we have—He is the Father of our Lord Jesus Christ, the source of every mercy, and the One Who so wonderfully comforts and strengthens us in our hardships and trials.

4 And why does He do this? That when others are troubled, needing our sympathy and encouragement, we can pass on to them this same help and comfort God has given us.

5 You can be sure that the more Christ shares His sufferings with us, the more He will shower us with His kindness and mercy, too.

6 So when I suffer it is for your good, to help you find Him Who gives salvation and comfort for your every need, and ours. When I am comforted by God, that, too, is for your good, for then I can show you from personal experience how God will tenderly comfort and deliver you from your troubles.

7 I know this: that the more you suffer, the more God will bless you, and help you, and give you His joy.

8 I think you ought to know, dear brothers, about the hard time I went through in Asia. I was in fact crushed, overwhelmed and desperate. I feared I would never live through it.

9 I felt I was doomed to die and saw how powerless I was to help myself; but that was good, for then I put everything into the hands of God, Who alone could save me, for He can even raise the dead.

10 And He did help me, and saved me from a terrible death; yes, and I expect Him to do it again and again.

11 But you must help me too, by praying for me. For much thanks and praise will go to God from those who see His wonderful answers to their prayers for my safety!

12 I am so glad that I can say with utter honesty that in all my dealings I have been pure and sincere, quietly depending upon the Lord for His help, and not on my own skill. And that is even more true, if possible, about the way I have acted towards you.

13, 14 My letters have been straightforward and sincere, and contain nothing but what you know is true. I trust that you will always accept and believe these truths, and that you can accept me and be proud of me, as you already are to some extent, just as I shall be of you on that day when our Lord Jesus comes back again.

15, 16 It was because I was so sure of your understanding and trust that I planned to stop and see you on my way to Macedonia, as well as afterwards when I was on my way to Judaea, so that I could be a double blessing to you.

17 Then why, you may be asking, did I change my plan? Hadn't I really made up my mind yet? Or am I like a man of the world who says "yes" when he really means "no"?

18 Never! As surely as God is true, I am not that sort of person. My "yes" means "yes."

19 Timothy and Silvanus and I have been telling you about Jesus Christ the Son of God. He isn't one to say "yes" when He means "no." He always does exactly what He says.

20 He carries out and fulfills all of God's promises, no matter how many of them there are; and we have told everyone how faithful He is, giving glory to His name.

21 It is this God Who has joined us together as parts of Christ's body, and given us each our special work to do.

22 He has put His brand upon us—His mark of ownership—and given us His Holy Spirit as proof that we belong to Him.

23 I call upon this God to witness against me if I am not telling the absolute truth: the reason I didn't come to visit you on my way to Macedonia was that I would have had to sadden you with a severe rebuke.

24 When I come, although I can't do much to help your faith, for it is strong already, I want to be able to do something about your joy: I want to make you happy, not sad.

CHAPTER 2

"No," I said to myself, "I won't do it. I'll not make them unhappy with another painful visit."

2 For if I make you sad, who is going to make me happy? You are the ones to do it, and how can you if I cause you pain?

3 That is why I wrote as I did in my last letter, so that you would have time to get things straightened out before I came. Then, when I do come, I will not be made sad by the very ones who ought to give me greatest joy. I felt sure that your happiness was so bound up in mine that you would not be happy either, unless I came with joy.

4 Oh, how I hated to write that letter! It almost broke my heart and I tell you honestly that I cried about it. I didn't want to hurt you but I had to show you how very much I loved you and cared about what was happening to you.

5 Remember that the man I wrote about, who caused all the trouble, has not caused sorrow to me as much as to all the rest of you—though I certainly have my share in it too.

6 I don't want to be harder on him than I should. He has been punished enough by your united disapproval.

7 Now it is time to forgive him and comfort him. Otherwise he may become so sad and discouraged that he won't be able to recover.

8 Please show him now that you still do love him very much.

9 I wrote to you as I did so that I could find out how far you would go in obeying me.

10 When you forgive anyone, I do too. And whatever I have forgiven, (for this affected me too), has been by Christ's authority. I knew you would want me to do this.

11 A further reason for forgiveness is that we will not be outsmarted by Satan; for we know what he is trying to do.

12 Well, when I got as far as the city of Troas, the Lord gave me tremendous opportunities to preach the Gospel.

13 But Titus, my dear brother, wasn't there to meet me and I couldn't rest, wondering where he was and what had happened to him. So I said goodby and went right on to Macedonia to try to find him, without stopping to see you.

14 But thanks be to God! For through what Christ has done, He has triumphed over all our stumbling efforts and uncertainties, and wherever we go He uses us to tell others about the Lord and to spread the Gospel like a sweet perfume.

15 As far as God is concerned there is a sweet, wholesome smell about us. It is the fragrance of Christ within us, and both the saved and unsaved all around us smell it, too.

16 To those who are not saved, we seem a fearful smell of death and doom, while to those who know Christ we are a life-giving perfume. But who is adequate for such a task as this? Who is able to do it as it should be done?

17 Only those who, like ourselves, are men of

truth, sent by God, speaking with Christ's power, with God's eye upon us. We are not like those—and there are many of them—whose idea in getting out the Gospel is to make a good living out of it.

CHAPTER 3

Are we beginning to be like those false teachers of yours who must tell you all about themselves and bring long letters of recommendation with them? I think you hardly need someone's letter to tell you about us, do you? And we don't need a recommendation from you, either!

2 The only letter I need is you, yourselves! By looking at the good change in your hearts, everyone can see that we have done a good work among you.

3 They can see that you are a letter from Christ, which we are showing to them. It is not a letter written with pen and ink, but by the Spirit of the living God, and not carved on stone, but in human hearts.

4 We dare to say these good things about ourselves only because of our great trust in God through Christ, that He will help us do them,

5 And not because we think we can do anything of lasting value by ourselves. Our only power and success comes from God.

6 He is the one Who has helped us show others His new plan for saving them. We do not tell them they must obey every law of God or die; but we tell them there is life for them from the Holy Spirit. The old way, trying to be saved by keeping the Ten Com-

mandments, ends in death; in the new way, the Holy Spirit gives them life.

7 Yet that old system of law that ended in death began with such glory that people could not bear to look at Moses' face. For, as he gave them God's law to obey, his face shone out with the very glory of God—though the brightness soon began to fade away.

8 Shall we not expect far greater glory in these days when the Holy Spirit is giving life?

9 If the plan that leads to doom was glorious, much more glorious is the plan that makes men right with God.

10. In fact, that first glory as shown in Moses' face is worth nothing at all in comparison with Christ's overwhelming glory.

11 If the old system that came to an end was full of heavenly glory, the glory we have now is surely far greater, for it goes on forever.

12 Since we know that this new glory will never go away, we can preach with great boldness,

13 And not as Moses did, who put a veil over his face so no one could see the glory fade away.

14 Not only Moses' face was veiled, but his people's minds and understanding were veiled and blinded too. Even now when the Old Testament is read it seems as though Jewish hearts and minds are covered by a thick veil, so that they cannot see and understand that the glory of the old system is gone, and that Christ's death for us has made the old plan out-of-date and worthless.

15 Yes, even today when they read Moses' writings

their hearts are blind and they think that obeying the Ten Commandments is the way to be saved.

16 Whenever anyone turns to the Lord from his sins, then the veil is taken away.

17 The Lord is the Spirit Who gives them life, and where He is there is freedom from trying to be saved by keeping the laws of God.

18 But we Christians have no veil over our faces; we can be mirrors that brightly reflect the glory of the Lord. As the Spirit of the Lord works within us, we become more and more like Him, and reflect Him more and more brightly.

CHAPTER 4

It is God Himself, in His mercy, Who has given us this wonderful work of telling His Good News to others, and so we never give up.

2 We do not try to trick people into believing—we denounce any preacher who uses such methods. We are not interested in fooling anyone; we never try to get anyone to think that the Bible teaches what it doesn't. We stand in the presence of God as we speak and so we tell the truth, as all who know us will agree.

3 If the Gospel is hidden to anyone, it shows that he is on the road to eternal death.

4 Satan has made him blind so that he will not see the glorious light of the Gospel that is shining upon him, and so that he will not understand the amazing message we preach about the glory of Christ, Who is God.

5 We don't go around preaching about ourselves, but about Christ Jesus as Lord. All we say of ourselves is that we are your slaves because of what Jesus has done for us.

6 For God, Who said, "Let there be light in the darkness," has made us understand the glory of God that is seen in the face of Jesus Christ.

7 But this precious treasure, this light and power within us is, as it were, in an old crockery bowl, that is, in our weak bodies. Everyone can see that the glorious power within must be from God and is not our own.

8 We are pressed on every side by troubles, but not crushed and broken. We are perplexed because we don't know why things happen as they do, but we don't give up and quit.

9 We are hunted down, but God never abandons us. We get knocked down, but we get up again and keep going.

10 These bodies of ours are constantly facing death just as Jesus did; so it is clear to all that it is only the living Christ within Who keeps us safe.

11 Yes, we live under constant danger to our lives because we serve the Lord, but this gives us constant opportunities to show forth the power of Jesus Christ within our dying bodies.

12 Because of our preaching we face death, but it has resulted in eternal life for you.

13 We boldly say what we believe, trusting God to care for us, just as the Psalm writer did when he said, "I believe and therefore I speak."

14 We know that the same God Who brought the

Lord Jesus back from death will also bring us back to life again with Jesus, and present us to Him along with you.

15 These sufferings of ours are for your benefit. And the more of you who are won to Christ, the more there are to thank Him for His great kindness, and the more the Lord is glorified.

16 That is why we never give up. It is hard on our health, but good for our souls. Down inside we grow stronger in the Lord every day.

17 These troubles and sufferings of ours are, after all, quite small and won't last very long. Yet this short time of distress will result in God's richest blessing upon us forever and ever!

18 So we do not look at what we can see down here, the troubles all around us, but we look forward to the joys in heaven which we have not yet seen. The troubles will soon go away, but the joys to come will last forever.

CHAPTER 5

For we know that when this tent we live in now is taken down—when we die and leave these bodies—we have a wonderful new home waiting for us up in heaven, a home that will be ours forevermore, made for us by God Himself, and not by human hands.

2 How weary we grow of these bodies down here; that is why we look forward eagerly to the day when we shall have heavenly bodies which we shall put on like new clothes.

3 For we shall not be merely spirits without bodies.

4 While we are still in these bodies down here, they make us groan and sigh, but we wouldn't like to think of dying and having no bodies at all. We want to slip into our new bodies so that these dying bodies will, as it were, be swallowed up by everlasting life.

5 That is what God has arranged for us and, as a guarantee, He has given us His Holy Spirit.

6 Now we look forward with confidence to our heavenly bodies and realize that every moment we are still down here means that much longer we must be away from heaven, where Jesus is.

7 We know these things are true by believing, not by seeing.

8 And we are not afraid, but are glad to be rid of these bodies, for then we will be at home with the Lord.

9 So our aim is to please Him always in everything we do, whether we are here in this body or away from this body and with Him in heaven.

10 For we must all stand before Christ to be judged. Each of us will receive the payment he deserves for the good or bad things he has done in these bodies here on earth.

11 It is because of this solemn fear of God ever present in our minds that we work so hard to win others. God knows our hearts, that they are pure in this matter, and I hope that, deep within, you really know it, too.

12 Are we trying to pat ourselves on the back again? No, I am giving you some good ammunition! You can use this on those preachers of yours who brag about how well they look and preach, but don't have true and honest hearts. You can say that we at least are honest.

13 Are we insane to say such things about ourselves? If so, it is to bring glory to God. And if we are in our right minds, it is for your benefit.

14 Whatever we do, it is certainly not for our own profit, but because Christ's love controls us now.

15 He died for all so that all who live—having received eternal life from Him—might live no longer for themselves, to please themselves, but to spend their lives pleasing Christ Who died and rose again for them.

16 So do not any longer estimate the value of Christians by what the world thinks about them or by what they seem to be like on the outside. Once I mistakenly thought of Christ that way, merely as a human being like myself. How differently I feel now!

17 When someone becomes a Christian he becomes a brand new person inside. He is not the same any more. A new life has begun!

18 All these new things are from God Who brought us back to Himself through what Christ Jesus did. And God has given us the privilege of urging everyone to come into His favor.

19 For God was in Christ, restoring the world to Himself, no longer counting men's sins against them but blotting them out. He has given us this wonderful message to tell others.

20 We are Christ's ambassadors. God is using us to speak to you: we beg you, as though Christ Himself were here pleading with you, receive the love He offers you.

21 For God took the sinless Christ and poured into Him our sins. Then, in exchange, He poured God's goodness into us!

CHAPTER 6

As God's partners we beg you not to toss aside this marvelous message of God's great kindness.

2 For God says, "Your cry came to me at a favorable time, when the doors of welcome were wide open. I helped you on a day when salvation was being offered." Right now God is ready to welcome you. Today He is ready to save you.

3 We try to live in such a way that no one will ever be offended or kept back from finding the Lord by the way we act, so that no one can find fault with us and blame it on the Lord.

4 In fact, in everything we do we try to show that we are true ministers of God. We patiently endure suffering and hardship and trouble of every kind.

5 We have been beaten, put in jail, faced angry mobs, worked to exhaustion, stayed awake through sleepless nights of watching, and gone without food.

6 We have proved ourselves to be what we claim by our wholesome lives and by our understanding of the Gospel and by our patience. We have been kind and loving and filled with the Holy Spirit.

7 We have been truthful, with God's power helping us in all we do. The weapons of a godly man have all been ours.

8 We stand true to the Lord whether others honor us or despise us, whether they criticize us or commend us. We are honest, but they call us liars.

9 The world ignores us, but we are known to God; we live close to death, but here we are, still very much

alive. We have gone through many difficulties, but God has kept us through them all.

10 Our hearts ache, but at the same time we have the joy of the Lord. We are poor, but we give rich spiritual gifts to others. We own nothing, and yet we enjoy everything.

11 Oh, my dear friends, there in Corinth! I have told you all my feelings; I love you with all my heart.

12 Any coldness between us is not because of any lack of love on my part. No, it is because your own love is so small that it does not reach to me.

13 I am talking to you now as if you truly were my very own children. Open your hearts! Enlarge your love!

14 Don't be chained to those who do not love the Lord, for what do the people of God have in common with the people of sin? How can light live with darkness?

15 And what harmony can there be between Christ and the devil? How can a Christian be a partner with one who scoffs at his faith?

16 And what connection can there be between God's temple and an idol temple? For you are God's temple, the home of the living God, and God has said of you, "I will live in them and walk among them, and I will be their God and they shall be my people."

17 That is why the Lord has said, "Come away from among them and stay away; touch not their evil things and I will welcome you,

18 "And be a Father to you, and you will be my sons and daughters," says our Almighty Lord.

CHAPTER 7

Having such great promises as these, dear friends, let us turn away from everything wrong, whether of body or spirit, and purify ourselves, living in the wholesome fear of God, giving ourselves to Him alone.

2 Please open your hearts to us again, for not one of you has suffered any wrong from us. Not one of you was led astray. We have cheated no one nor taken advantage of anyone.

3 I'm not saying this to scold or blame you, for, as I have said before, you are in my heart forever and I live and die with you.

4 I have the highest confidence in you, and my pride in you is great. You are such a comfort to me; you make me so happy in spite of all my suffering.

5 When we arrived in Macedonia there was no rest for us; trouble was on every hand and all around us; inside, our hearts were full of dread and fear.

6 Then God Who cheers those who are discouraged refreshed us by sending Titus.

7 Not only was his presence a joy, but also the news that he brought of the wonderful time he had with you. When he told me how much you were looking forward to my visit, and how sorry you were about what had happened, and about your loyalty and warm love for me, well, I overflowed with joy!

8 I am no longer sorry that I sent that letter to you, though I was very sorry for a time when I saw how much it hurt you. But it hurt you only for a little while.

9 Now I am glad I sent it, not because it hurt you,

but because the hurt turned you to God. It was a good kind of sorrow I gave you, a godly sorrow, not something that harmed you.

10 For when we allow God to use sorrow in our lives it helps us turn away from sin and seek eternal life. We should never regret His sending it. But the sorrow of the man who is not a Christian is hopeless and deadly, for it reflects his eternal loss.

11 Just see how much good this grief from the Lord did for you! You no longer shrugged your shoulders, but became earnest and sincere, and very anxious to get rid of the sin that I wrote you about. You became frightened about what had happened, and longed for me to come and help. You went right to work on the problem and cleared it up, punishing the man who sinned. You have done everything you could to make it right.

12 I wrote as I did so the Lord could show how much you really do care for us. That was my purpose even more than to help the man who sinned, or his father to whom he did the wrong.

13 In addition to the encouragement you gave us by your love, we were made happier still by Titus' joy when he had such a wonderful time with you.

14 I told him how it would be—told him before he left me of my pride in you—and you didn't disappoint me. I have always told you the truth and now my boasting to Titus has also proved true!

15 He loves you more than ever when he remembers the way you listened to him so willingly and received him so anxiously and with such deep concern.

16 How happy this makes me, now that I am sure

all is well between us again. Once again I can have perfect confidence in you.

CHAPTER 8

Now I want to tell you about the way God has been leading the churches in Macedonia.

2 Though they have been going through much trouble and deep waters, they have mixed their wonderful joy with their deep poverty, and the result has been an overflow of giving to others.

3 They gave not only what they could afford, but far more; and I can testify that they did it because they wanted to, and not because of nagging on my part.

4 They begged us to take the money so they could share in the joy of helping the Christians in Jerusalem.

5 Best of all, they went beyond our highest hopes, for their first action was to rededicate themselves to the Lord and to us, for whatever directions God might give to them through us.

6 They were so enthusiastic about it that we have urged Titus, who has already done so much among you, to visit you and encourage you to share in this ministry of giving.

7 You people there are leaders in so many ways—you have so much faith, so many good preachers, so much learning, so much enthusiasm, so much love for us. Now I want you to be leaders also in the spirit of cheerful giving.

8 I am not giving you an order; I am not saying you must do it, but others are eager for it. This is

a way to prove that your love is real, that it goes beyond mere words.

9 You know how full of love and kindness our Lord Jesus was: though He was very rich, yet to help you He became very poor, so that by being poor He could make you very rich.

10 I want to suggest that you finish what you started to do a year ago, for you were not only the first to propose this idea, but the first to begin doing something about it.

11 Having started the ball rolling so enthusiastically, you should carry it through to completion just as gladly, giving whatever you can, out of whatever you have. Let your enthusiastic idea at the start be equalled by your realistic action now.

12 If you are really eager to give, then it isn't important how much you have to give. God wants you to give what you have, not what you haven't.

13 I don't mean, either, that those who receive your gifts should have an easy time of it at your expense,

14 But you should divide with them. Right now you have plenty and can help them. Then at some other time they can share with you when you need it, and so each will have as much as he needs.

15 Do you remember what the Scriptures say about this? "He that gathered much had nothing left over, and he that gathered little had enough."

16 I am thankful to God that He has given Titus the same real concern for you that I have.

17 He is glad to follow my suggestion that he visit

you again—but I think he would have come anyway, for he is very eager to see you!

18 I am sending another well-known brother with him, who is highly praised as a gospel preacher in all the churches.

19 In fact, this man was elected by the churches to travel with me to Jerusalem to help distribute the gift. This will glorify the Lord and show our eagerness to help each other.

20 By traveling together we will guard each other from any suspicion, for we are anxious that no one should find fault with the way we are handling this large gift.

21 God knows we are honest, but I want everyone else to know it, too. That is why we have made this arrangement.

22 And I am sending you still another brother, whom we know from experience to be an earnest Christian. He is especially interested, as he looks forward to this trip, because I have told him all about your eagerness to help.

23 If anyone asks who Titus is, say that he is my partner and my helper in helping you, and you can say that the two other men are sent by the churches, and that they are splendid examples of those who belong to the Lord.

24 Please show your love to these men and do for them all I have publicly boasted you would.

CHAPTER 9

I realize that I really don't even need to mention this to you, about helping God's people.

2 For I know how eager you are to do it, and I have boasted to the friends in Macedonia that you were ready to send an offering a year ago. In fact, it was this enthusiasm of yours that stirred up many of them to begin helping.

3 But I am sending these men just to be sure that you really are ready, as I told them you would be, with your money all collected; I don't want it to turn out that this time I was wrong in my boasting about you.

4 I would be very much ashamed—and so would you—if some of these Macedonian people come with me and find you still aren't ready after all I have told them!

5 So I have asked these other brethren to arrive ahead of me to see that the gift you promised is on hand and waiting. I want it to be a real gift and not look as if it were being given under pressure.

6 But remember this, that if you give little you will get little. A farmer who plants just a few seeds will get only a small crop, but if he plants much, he will reap much.

7 Every one must make up his own mind as to how much he should give. Don't force anyone to give more than he really wants to, for cheerful givers are the ones God prizes.

8 God is able to make it up to you by giving you everything you need and more, so that there will not only be enough for your own needs, but plenty left over to give joyfully to others.

9 It is as the Scriptures say: "You will be able to give much to the poor and your good deeds will honor you forever."

10 For God, Who gives seed to the farmer to plant, and later on, good crops to harvest and eat, will give you more and more seed to plant so that you can give away more and more fruit from your harvest.

11 Yes, God will give you much so that you can give away much, and when we take your gifts to those who need them they will break out into thanksgiving and praise to God for your help.

12 So, two good things happen as a result of your gifts—those in need are helped, and many overflow with thanks to God.

13 Those you help will be glad not only because of your generous gifts to themselves and to others, but they will praise God for this proof that you really do love the Lord.

14 And they will pray for you with deep fervor and feeling because of the wonderful grace of God within you.

15 Thank God for His Son—His Gift too wonderful for words.

CHAPTER 10

I plead with you—yes, I, Paul—but I plead gently, as Christ Himself would do. Yet some of you are saying, "Paul's letters are bold enough when he is far away, but when he gets here he will be afraid to raise his voice!"

2 I hope I won't need to show you when I come how harsh and rough I can be. I don't want to carry out my present plans against some of you who seem to

think my deeds and words are merely those of an ordinary man.

3 It is true that I am an ordinary weak human being, but I don't use human plans and methods to win my battles.

4 I use God's mighty weapons, not those made by men, to knock down the devil's strongholds.

5 These weapons can break down every proud argument against God and every wall that can be built to keep men from finding Him. With these weapons I can capture rebels and bring them back to God, and change them into men whose hearts' desire is obedience to Christ.

6 I will use these weapons against every rebel who remains after I have first used them on you, yourselves, and you surrender to Christ.

7 The trouble with you is that you look at me and I seem weak and powerless, but you don't look beneath the surface. Yet if anyone among you can claim the power and authority of Christ, I certainly can.

8 I am not in the least embarrassed by my strong claims of authority over you—authority to help you, not to hurt you—for these claims are all true.

9 I say this so that you will not think I am just blustering when I scold you in my letters.

10 "Don't bother about his letters," some say. "He sounds big, but it's all noise. When he gets here you will see that there is nothing great about him, and you have never heard a worse preacher!"

11 This time my personal presence is going to be just as rough on you as my letters are!

12 Oh, don't worry, I wouldn't dare say that I am as wonderful as these other men who tell you how good they are! Their trouble is that they are only comparing themselves with each other, and measuring themselves against their own little ideas.

13 Well, we are not like that, boasting without a yardstick to measure ourselves against. Our goal is to measure up to God's plan for us, and this plan includes our working there with you.

14 We are not going too far when we claim you as part of our work program, for we were the first to come to you with the Gospel of Christ.

15 We are not trying to claim credit for the work someone else has done among you. And when your faith is strong enough, I hope to go much farther still,

16 To other cities that are far beyond you, where no one else is working; then there will be no question about being in someone else's field.

17 If anyone is going to boast, let him boast about what the Lord has done and not about himself.

18 When someone boasts about himself—how well he has done—it doesn't count for much. But when the Lord says so, that's different!

CHAPTER 11

Would to God that you could be patient with me as I keep on talking like a fool. Do bear with me and let me say what is on my heart.

2 I am jealous for you with the deep concern of God Himself—jealous that your love should be for

Christ alone, just as a pure maiden gives her love to one man only, the one who will be her husband.

3 But I am frightened, fearing that in some way you will be led away from your pure and simple devotion to our Lord, as Eve was deceived by Satan in the Garden of Eden.

4 You seem so gullible: you believe whatever anyone tells you even if he is preaching about another Jesus than the One we preach, or a different spirit than the Holy Spirit you received, or shows you a different way to be saved. You swallow it all.

5 Yet I don't feel that these marvelous "messengers from God," as they call themselves, are any better than I am.

6 If I am a poor speaker, at least I know what I am talking about, as I think you realize by now, for we have proved it again and again.

7 Did I do wrong and cheapen myself and make you look down on me because I preached God's Good News to you without charging you anything?

8 Instead I "robbed" other churches by taking what they sent me, and using it up while I was with you, so that I could serve you without cost.

9 And when that was gone and I was getting hungry I still didn't ask you for anything, for the Christians from Macedonia brought me another gift. I have never yet asked you for one cent, and I never will.

10 I promise this with every ounce of truth I have in me that I will tell everyone in Greece about it!

11 Why? Because I don't love you? God knows I do.

12 But I will do it to cut out the ground from under

the feet of those who boast that they are doing God's work in just the same way we are.

13 God never sent these men at all; they are "phonies" who have fooled you into thinking they are Christ's apostles.

14 Yet I am not surprised! Satan can change himself into an angel of light,

15 So it is no wonder his servants can do it too, and seem like godly ministers. In the end they will get every bit of punishment their wicked deeds deserve.

16 Again I plead, don't think that I have lost my wits to talk like this; but even if you do, listen to me anyway—a witless man, a fool—while I boast a little as they do.

17 Such bragging isn't something the Lord commanded me to do, for I am acting like a brainless fool.

18 Yet these other men keep telling you how wonderful they are; so here I go:

19, 20 (You think you are so wise—yet you listen gladly to these fools; you don't mind at all when they make you their slaves and take everything you have, and take advantage of you, and put on airs, and slap you in the face.

21 I'm ashamed to say that I'm not strong and daring like that! But whatever they can boast about—I'm talking like a fool again—I can boast about it, too.)

22 They brag that they are Hebrews, do they? Well, so am I. And they say that they are Israelites, God's chosen people? So am I. And they are relatives of Abraham? Well, I am too.

23 They say they serve Christ? But I have served

Him far more! (Have I gone mad to boast like this?) I have worked harder, been put in jail oftener, been whipped times without number, and faced death again and again and again.

24 Five different times the Jews gave me their terrible thirty-nine lashes.

25 Three times I was beaten with rods. Once I was stoned. Three times I was shipwrecked. Once I was in the water all night and the whole next day.

26 I have traveled many weary miles and been often in great danger from flooded rivers and from robbers and from my own people, the Jews, as well as at the hands of the Gentiles. I have faced grave dangers from mobs in the cities and from death in the deserts and in the stormy seas and from men who claim to be brothers in Christ but are not.

27 I have lived with weariness and pain and sleepless nights. Often I have been hungry and thirsty and gone without food; often I have shivered with cold, without enough clothing to keep me warm.

28 Then, besides all this, I have the constant worry of how the churches are getting along:

29 Who makes a mistake and I do not feel his sadness? Who falls without my longing to help him? Who is spiritually hurt without my fury rising against the one who hurt him?

30 But if I must brag, I would rather brag about the things that show how weak I am.

31 God, the Father of our Lord Jesus Christ, Who is to be praised forever and ever, knows I tell the truth.

32 For instance, in Damascus the governor under

King Aretas kept guards at the city gates to catch me;

33 But I was let down in a basket from a hole in the city wall, and so I got away! What popularity!

CHAPTER 12

This boasting is all so foolish, but let me go on. Let me tell about the visions I've had, and revelations from the Lord.

2, 3 Fourteen years ago I was taken up to heaven for a visit. Don't ask me whether my body was there or just my spirit, for I don't know; only God can answer that. But anyway, there I was in paradise,

4 And heard things so astounding that they are beyond a man's power to describe or put in words (and anyway I am not allowed to tell them to others).

5 That experience is something worth bragging about, but I am not going to do it. I am going to boast only about how weak I am and how great God is to use such weakness for His glory.

6 I have plenty to boast about and would be no fool in doing it, but I don't want anyone to think more highly of me than he should from what he can actually see in my life and my message.

7 I will say this: because these experiences I had were so tremendous, God was afraid I might be puffed up by them; so there was given me a sickness which has been a thorn in my flesh, a messenger from Satan to hurt and bother me, and prick my pride.

8 Three different times I begged God to make me well again.

9 Each time He said, "No. But I am with you;

that is all you need. My power shows up best in weak people." Now I am glad to boast about how weak I am; I am glad to be a living demonstration of Christ's power, instead of showing off my own power and abilities.

10 Since I know it is all for Christ's good, I am quite happy about "the thorn," and about insults and hardships and persecutions; for when I am weak, then I am strong. The less I have, the more I depend on Him.

11 You have made me act like a fool, boasting, for you people ought to be writing about me and not making me write about myself. There isn't a single thing these other marvelous fellows have that I don't have too, even though I am really worth nothing at all.

12 When I was there I certainly gave you every proof that I was truly an apostle, sent to you by God Himself: for I patiently did many wonders and signs and mighty works among you.

13 The only thing I didn't do for you, that I do everywhere else in all other churches, was to become a burden to you—I didn't ask you to give me food to eat and a place to stay. Please forgive me for this wrong!

14 Now I am coming to you again, the third time; and it is still not going to cost you anything, for I don't want your money. I want *you!* And anyway, you are my children, and little children don't pay for their father's and mother's food; it's the other way around. Fathers and mothers buy the food for their children.

15 I am glad to give you myself and all I have to help you grow, even though it seems like the more I love you, the less you love me.

16 Some of you are saying, "It's true that his visits

didn't seem to cost us anything, but he is a sneaky fellow, that Paul, and he fooled us. As sure as anything he must have made some money off us some way."

17 But how? Did any of the men I sent to help you get anything from you?

18 When I begged Titus to visit you, and sent our other brother with him, did they make any profit? No, of course not. For we have the same Holy Spirit, and walk in each other's steps, doing things the same way.

19 I suppose you think I am saying all this to get back into your good graces. That isn't it at all. I tell you, with God listening as I say it, that I have said this to help *you*—to build you up spiritually—and not to help myself.

20 For I am afraid that when I come to visit you I won't like what I find, and then you won't like the way I will need to act. I am afraid that I will find you quarreling, and envying each other, and being angry with each other, and acting big, and saying wicked things about each other, whispering behind each other's backs, and that you will be loud and coarse.

21 Yes, I am afraid that when I come God will humble me and I will be sad and embarrassed because of some of those who have sinned and don't even care about the wicked, impure things they have done: their lust and immorality, and the taking of other men's wives.

CHAPTER 13

This is the third time I am coming to visit you. The Scriptures tell us that if two or three have seen a wrong, it must be punished. Well, this is my third warning, as I come now for this visit.

2 I have already warned those who had been sinning when I was there last; now I warn them again, and all others, just as I did then, that this time I come ready to punish severely and I will not spare them.

3 I will give you all the proof you want that Christ speaks through me. Christ is not weak in His dealings with you, but is a mighty power within you.

4 His weak, human body died on the cross, but now He lives by the mighty power of God; we, too, are weak in our bodies, as He was, but now we live and are strong, as He is, and have all of God's power to use.

5 Check up on yourselves. Are you really Christians? Do you pass the test? Do you feel Christ's presence and power more and more within you? Or are you just pretending to be Christians when actually God has rejected you?

6 I hope you can agree that we have stood that test and truly belong to the Lord.

7 I pray that you will live good lives, not because that will be a feather in our caps, proving that what we teach is right; no, for we want you to do right even if we are despised.

8 Our responsibility is to encourage the right at all times, not to hope for evil.

9 We are glad to be weak and despised if you are really strong; our greatest wish and prayer is that you will become mature Christians.

10 I am writing this to you now in the hope that I won't need to scold and punish when I come; for I want to use God's power which He has given me to make you strong, not to punish you.

11 I close my letter with these last words:

1. Rejoice.
2. Grow up in Christ.
3. Be comforted.
4. Live in harmony and peace.

And may the God of love and peace be with you.

12 Greet each other warmly in the Lord.

13 All the Christians here send you their best regards.

14 May the grace of our Lord Jesus Christ be with you all. May God's love and the Holy Spirit's friendship be yours.

Paul

Galatians

CHAPTER 1

From: Paul the missionary and all the other Christians here.

To: The Churches of Galatia.

The message I bring you is no ordinary one; for it is not from other men but from Jesus Christ Himself, and from God the Father Who raised Him from the dead.

3 May peace and blessing be yours from God the Father and from Jesus Christ our Lord.

4 He died for our sins just as God our Father planned, and made a way for us to escape from this evil world in which we live.

5 All glory to God through all the ages of eternity. Amen.

6 I am astounded that you have turned away so quickly from the truth. God invited you to share the eternal life He gives through Christ; and now you are already following a different "way to heaven," which really doesn't go to heaven at all.

7 For there is no other way than the one we showed you; you are being fooled by those who twist and change the truth concerning Christ.

8 Let God's curses fall on anyone, including myself, who preaches any other way to be saved than the one

we told you about; yes, if an angel comes from heaven and preaches any other message, let him be forever cursed.

9 I will say it again: if anyone preaches any other Gospel than the one you heard from us, let God's curse fall upon him.

10 You can see that I am not trying to please you by sweet talk and flattery; no, I am trying to please God. If I tried to please men I could not be Christ's servant.

11 Dear friends, I solemnly swear that the way to heaven which I preach is not based on some mere human whim or dream.

12 For my message comes from no less a Person than Jesus Christ Himself, Who told me what to say. No one else has taught me.

13 You know what I was like when I followed the Jewish religion—how I went after the Christians mercilessly, hunting them down and doing my best to get rid of them all.

14 I was one of the most religious Jews of my own age in the whole country, and tried as hard as I possibly could to follow all the old, traditional rules of my religion.

15 But then something happened! For even before I was born God had chosen me to be His, and called me—what kindness and grace—

16 To put His Son within me so that I could go to the Gentiles and show them the Good News about Jesus. When all this happened to me I didn't go and talk it over with anyone else;

17 I didn't go up to Jerusalem to consult with those

who were apostles before I was. No, I went away into the deserts of Arabia, and then came back to the city of Damascus.

18 It was not until three years later that I finally went to Jerusalem for a visit with Peter, and stayed there with him for fifteen days.

19 And the only other apostle I met at that time was James, our Lord's brother.

20 (Listen to what I am saying, for I am telling you this in the very presence of God. This is exactly what happened—I am not lying to you.)

21 Then after this visit I went to Syria and Cilicia.

22 But the Christians in Judea still didn't even know what I looked like.

23 All they knew was what people were saying, that "our former enemy is now preaching the very faith he tried to wreck."

24 And they gave glory to God because of me.

CHAPTER 2

Then after fourteen years I went back to Jerusalem again, this time with Barnabas; and Titus came along too.

2 I went there because of definite orders from God to talk with the brethren about the message I preach to the Gentiles. I talked privately to the leaders of the church so that they would all understand just what I had been teaching and, I hoped, agree that it was right.

3 And they did agree; they did not even demand

that Titus, my companion, should be circumcised, though he was a Gentile.

4 Even that question wouldn't have come up except for some "Christians" there—false ones, really—who came to spy on us and see what freedom we enjoyed in Christ Jesus, as to whether we obeyed the Jewish laws or not. They tried to get us all tied up in their rules, like slaves in chains.

5 But we did not listen to them for a single moment, for we did not want to confuse you into thinking that salvation can be earned by being circumcised and by obeying Jewish laws.

6 And the great leaders of the church who were there had nothing to add to what I was preaching. (By the way, their being great leaders made no difference to me, for all are the same to God.)

7, 8, 9 And when Peter, James and John, who seemed to be the pillars of the church, saw how greatly God had used me in winning the Gentiles, just as Peter had been blessed so greatly in his preaching to the Jews—for the same God gave us each our special gifts—they gave Barnabas and me the right hand of fellowship. They encouraged us to keep right on with our preaching to the Gentiles while they continued their work with the Jews.

10 The only thing they did suggest was that we must always remember to help the poor, and I too am eager for that.

11 But when Peter came to Antioch I had to oppose him, speaking sharply to him because what he did was very wrong.

12 For when he first arrived he ate with the Gen-

tile Christians who don't bother with circumcision and other Jewish laws. But afterwards when some Jewish friends of James came, he wouldn't eat with the Gentiles anymore because he was afraid of what these friends of James would say;

13 And then all the other Jewish Christians and even Barnabas followed Peter's example, though they knew better.

14 When I saw what was happening and that they weren't being honest about what they really believed, and weren't following the truth of the Gospel, I said to Peter in front of all the others, "You are a Jew, and yet you haven't been obeying the Jewish laws; so why, all of a sudden, are you trying to make these Gentiles obey them?

15 You and I are Jews by birth, not mere Gentile sinners,

16 And yet we Jewish Christians know very well that we cannot become right with God by obeying our Jewish laws, but only by faith in Jesus Christ to take away our sins. And so we too have trusted Jesus Christ, that we might be accepted by God because of faith—and not because we have obeyed the Jewish laws. For no one will ever be saved by obeying them."

17 (But what if we trust Christ to save us and then find that we are wrong, and that we cannot be saved without being circumcised and obeying all the other Jewish laws? Wouldn't we need to say that faith in Christ had ruined us? God forbid that anyone should dare to think such things about our Lord.

18 Rather, we are sinners if we start building up

again the false idea we once destroyed, of being saved by keeping Jewish laws.

19 For the Old Testament itself leads me on to Christ, and shows me that its laws do not apply to me—they are not the way of my salvation—and so I am free to live for God.)

20 I have been crucified with Christ: and I myself no longer live, but Christ lives in me. And the real life I now have within this body is a result of my trusting in the Son of God, Who loved me and gave Himself for me.

21 I am not one of those who treats Christ's death as meaningless. For if we could be saved by keeping Jewish laws, then there was no need for Christ to die.

CHAPTER 3

Oh foolish Galatians! What magician has put a charm on you? For you used to see so clearly all I told you about the meaning of Jesus Christ's death.

2 Let me ask you this one question: Did you receive the Holy Spirit by trying to keep the Jewish laws? Of course not, for the Holy Spirit came upon you only after you heard about Christ and trusted Him to save you.

3 Then have you gone completely crazy? For if trying to obey the Jewish laws never gave you spiritual life in the first place, why do you think that trying to obey them now will make you stronger Christians?

4 You have suffered so much for the Gospel. Now are you going to just throw it all overboard? I can hardly believe it!

5 I ask you again, does God give you the power of

the Holy Spirit and work miracles among you as a result of your trying to obey the Jewish laws? No, of course not. It is when you believe in Christ and fully trust Him.

6 Abraham had the same experience. For God declared him fit for heaven only because he believed God's promises.

7 You can see from this that the real children of Abraham are all the men of faith who truly trust in God.

8 What's more, the Scriptures looked forward to this time when God would save the Gentiles also, through their faith. God told Abraham about this long ago when He said, "I will bless those in every nation who trust in me as you do."

9 And so it is: all who trust in Christ share the same blessing Abraham received.

10 Yes, and those who depend on the Jewish laws to save them are under God's curse, for the Scriptures say very clearly, "Cursed is everyone who at any time breaks a single one of these laws that are written in God's Book of the Law."

11 Consequently it is clear that no one can ever win God's favor by trying to keep the Jewish laws, because God has said that the only way we can be right in His sight is by faith.

12 How different from this way of faith is the way of law which says that a man is saved by obeying every law of God, without one slip.

13 But Christ has bought us out from under the doom of that impossible system by taking the curse for our wrong-doing upon Himself. For it is written in the

Old Testament, "Anyone who is hanged on a tree is cursed" (as Jesus was on the wooden cross).†

* * * * *

14 Now God can bless the Gentiles too, with this same blessing He promised to Abraham; and all of us as Christians can have the promised Holy Spirit through this faith.

15 Dear brothers, even in everyday life a promise made by one man to another, if it is written down and signed, cannot be changed. He cannot decide afterward to do something else instead.

16 Now a promise was made by God to Abraham and his Child. And notice that it doesn't say the promise was to his *children,* as it would if all his sons—all the Jews—were being spoken of, but to his *Child*—and that of course means Christ.

17 Here's what I am trying to say: God's promise to save through faith—and God wrote this promise down and signed it—could not be canceled or changed four hundred and thirty years later when God gave the Ten Commandments.

18 If obeying those laws could save us, then it is obvious that we would not be saved in the same way Abraham was, by accepting God's promise.

19 Well then, why were the laws given? They were added, after the promise was given, to show men they are guilty and in need of God's help that comes from having faith. But this system of law was to last only until the coming of Christ, the Child to whom God's promise was made. (And there is this further difference:

†implied

God gave His laws to angels to give to Moses, who then gave them to the people;

20 But when God gave His promise to Abraham, He did it by Himself alone, without angels or Moses in between.)

21 Well then, are God's laws and God's promises against each other? Of course not! If we could be saved by His laws, then God would not have had to give us a different way.

22 But the Scriptures tell us that no one has ever yet kept God's laws; all have sinned by breaking them, and so no one is saved by obeying them. The only way left to get what God promised is through faith in Jesus Christ, and the promises are given to all who believe Him.

23 Until Christ came we were guarded by the law, kept in protective custody, so to speak, until we could be delivered over to faith in the Saviour Who was coming.

24 Let me put it another way. The Jewish laws were our teacher and guide to lead us to Christ, so that we could be given right standing with God through our faith.

25 But now we have come to Christ and we don't need those laws any longer to guard us and lead us to Him.

26 For now you are all children of God through faith in Jesus Christ,

27 And you who have been baptized into Christ have become like Him.

28 You are no longer Jews or Greeks or slaves or free men or even merely men or women, but you

are all the same—you are Christians, you are one in Christ Jesus.

29 And now that you are Christ's you are the true children of Abraham, and all of God's promises to him belong to you.

CHAPTER 4

But remember this, that if a father dies and leaves great wealth for his little son, that child is not much better off than a slave until he grows up, even though he actually owns everything his father had.

2 He has to do what his guardians and managers tell him to, until he reaches whatever age his father set.

3 And that is the way it was with us before Christ came. We were slaves to Jewish laws and rituals for we thought they could save us.

4 But when the right time came, the time God decided on, He sent His Son, born of a woman, born as a Jew,

5 To buy freedom for us who were slaves to the law so that He could adopt us as His very own sons.

6 And because we are His sons God has sent the Spirit of His Son into our hearts so that we can rightly speak of God as our dear Father.

7 Now we are no longer slaves, but God's own sons. And since we are His sons, everything He has belongs to us, for that is the way God planned.

8 Before you Gentiles knew God you were slaves to so-called gods that did not even exist.

9 And now that you have found God (or I should

say, now that God has found you) how can it be that you want to go back again and become slaves once more to another poor, weak, useless religion of trying to get to heaven by obeying God's laws?

10 You are trying to find favor with God by what you do or don't do on certain days or months or seasons or years.

11 I fear for you. I am afraid that all my hard work for you was worth nothing.

12 Dear brothers, please feel as I do about these things, for I am as free from these chains as you used to be. You did not despise me then when I first preached to you,

13 Even though I was sick when I first brought you the Good News of Christ.

14 But even though my sickness was revolting to you, you didn't reject me and turn me away. No, you took me in and cared for me as though I were an angel from God, or even Jesus Christ Himself.

15 Where is that happy spirit that we felt together then? For in those days I know you would gladly have taken out your own eyes and given them to replace mine if that would have helped me.

16 And now have I become your enemy because I tell you the truth?

17 These false teachers who are so anxious to win your favor are not doing it for your own good. What they are trying to do is to shut you off from me so that you will pay more attention to them.

18 It is a fine thing when people are nice to you

with good motives and sincere hearts, especially if they aren't doing it just when I am with you!

19 Oh my children, how you are hurting me. I am once again suffering for you the pains of a mother waiting for her child to be born—longing for the time when you will finally be filled with Christ.

20 How I wish I could be there with you right now and not have to reason with you like this, for at this distance I frankly don't know what to do.

21 Listen to me, you friends who think you have to obey the Jewish laws to be saved: Why don't you find out what those laws really mean?

22 For it is written that Abraham had two sons, one from his slave-wife and one from his freeborn wife.

23 There was nothing unusual about the birth of the slave-wife's baby. But the baby of the freeborn wife was born only after God had especially promised he would come.

24, 25 Now this true story is an illustration of God's two ways of helping people. One way was by giving them His laws to obey. He did this on Mount Sinai, when He gave the Ten Commandments to Moses. Mount Sinai, by the way, is called "Mount Hagar" by the Arabs—and in my illustration Abraham's slave-wife Hagar represents Jerusalem, the mother-city of the Jews, the center of that system of trying to please God by obeying God's laws; and the Jews, who try to follow that system, are her slave children.

26 But our mother-city is the heavenly Jerusalem, and she is not a slave to Jewish laws.

27 That is what Isaiah meant when he prophesied,

"Now you can rejoice, oh childless woman; you can shout with joy though you never before had a child. For I am going to give you many children—more children than the slave-wife has."

28 You and I, dear brothers, are the children that God promised, just as Isaac was.

29 And so we who are born of the Holy Spirit are persecuted now by those who want us to keep the Jewish laws, just as Isaac the child of promise was persecuted by Ishmael the slave-girl's son.

30 But the Scriptures say that God told Abraham to send away the slave-wife and her son, for the slave-wife's son could not inherit Abraham's home and lands along with the free woman's son.

31 Dear brothers, we are not slave children, obligated to the Jewish laws, but children of the free woman, acceptable to God because of our faith.

CHAPTER 5

So Christ has made us free. Now make sure that you stay free and don't get all tied up again in the chains of slavery to Jewish laws and ceremonies.

2 Listen to me, for I really mean it: if you are counting on circumcision and keeping the Jewish laws to make you right with God, then Christ cannot save you.

3 I'll say it again. Anyone trying to find favor with God by being circumcised must always obey every other Jewish law or perish.

4 Christ is useless to you if you are counting on clearing your debt to God by keeping those laws; you are lost from God's grace.

5 But we by the help of the Holy Spirit are counting on Christ's death to clear away our sins and make us right with God.

6 And we to whom Christ has given eternal life don't need to worry about whether we have been circumcised or not, or whether we are obeying the Jewish ceremonies or not; for all we need is faith working through love.

7 You were getting along so well. Who has interfered with you to hold you back from following the truth?

8 It certainly isn't God Who has done it, for He is the one Who has called you to freedom in Christ.

9 But it only takes one wrong person among you to infect all the others.

10 I am trusting the Lord to bring you back to believing as I do about these things. God will deal with that person, whomever he is, who has been troubling and confusing you.

11 Some people even say that I myself am preaching that circumcision and Jewish laws are necessary to the plan of salvation. Well, if I preached that, I would be persecuted no more—for that message doesn't offend anyone. The fact that I am still being persecuted proves that I am still preaching salvation through faith in the cross of Christ alone.

12 I only wish these teachers who want you to cut yourselves by being circumcised would cut themselves off from you and leave you alone!

13 For, dear brothers, you have been given freedom: not freedom to do wrong, but freedom to love and serve each other.

14 For the whole Law can be summed up in this one command: "Love others as you love yourself."

15 But if instead of showing love among yourselves you are always critical and catty, watch out! Beware of ruining each other.

16 I advise you to obey only the Holy Spirit's instructions. He will tell you where to go and what to do, and then you won't always be doing the wrong things your evil nature wants you to.

17 For we naturally love to do evil things that are just the opposite from the things that the Holy Spirit tells us to do; and the good things we want to do when the Spirit has His way with us are just the opposite of our natural desires. These two forces within us are constantly fighting each other to win control over us and our wishes are never free from their pressures.

18 When you are guided by the Holy Spirit you need no longer force yourself to obey Jewish laws.

19 But when you follow your own wrong inclinations your lives will produce these evil results: impure thoughts; eagerness for lustful pleasure;

20 Idolatry, spiritism (that is, encouraging the activity of demons); hatred and fighting; jealousy and anger; constant effort to get the best for yourself; complaints and criticisms; the feeling that everyone else is wrong except those in your own little group; and there will be wrong doctrine,

21 Envy, murder, drunkenness, wild parties and all that sort of thing. Let me tell you again as I have before, that anyone living that sort of life will not inherit the kingdom of God.

22 But when the Holy Spirit controls our lives He

will produce this kind of fruit in us: love, joy, peace, patience, kindness, goodness, faithfulness,

23 Gentleness and self-control; and here there is no conflict with Jewish laws.

24 Those who belong to Chirst have nailed their natural evil desires to His cross and crucified them there.

25 If we are living now by the Holy Spirit's power, let us follow the Holy Spirit's leading in every part of our lives.

26 Then we won't need to look for honors and popularity, which lead to jealousy and hard feelings.

CHAPTER 6

Dear brothers, if a Christian is overcome by some sin, you who are godly should gently and humbly help him back onto the right path, remembering that next time it might be one of you who is in the wrong.

2 Share each other's troubles and problems, and so obey our Lord's command.

3 If anyone thinks he is too great to stoop to this, he is fooling himself. He is really a nobody.

4 Let everyone be sure that he is doing his very best, for then he will have the personal satisfaction of work well-done, and won't need to compare himself with someone else.

5 Each of us must bear some faults and burdens of his own. For none of us is perfect!

6 Those who are taught the Word of God should help their teachers by paying them.

7 Don't be misled; remember that you can't ignore God and get away with it: a man will always reap just the kind of crop he sows!

8 If he sows to please his own wrong desires, he will be planting seeds of evil and he will surely reap a harvest of spiritual decay and death; but if he plants the good things of the Spirit, he will reap the everlasting life which the Holy Spirit gives him.

9 And let us not get tired of doing what is right, for after a while we will reap a harvest of blessing if we don't get discouraged and give up.

10 That's why whenever we can we should always be kind to everyone, and especially to our Christian brothers.

11 I will write these closing words in my own handwriting. See how large I have to make the letters!

12 Those teachers of yours who are trying to force you to be circumcised are doing it for just one reason: so that they can be popular and avoid the persecution they would get if they admitted that the cross of Christ alone can save.

13 And even those teachers who submit to circumcision don't try to keep the other Jewish laws; but they want you to be circumcised in order that they can boast that you are their disciples.

14 But God forbid that I should boast about anything except the cross of our Lord Jesus Christ. Because of that cross my interest in all the attractive things of the world has been killed long ago, and the world's interest in me is also long dead.

15 It doesn't make any difference now whether we have been circumcised or not; what counts is whether

we really have been changed into new and different people.

16 May God's mercy and peace be upon all of you who live by this principle and upon those everywhere who are really God's own.

17 From now on please don't argue with me about these things, for I carry on my body the scars of the whippings and wounds from Jesus' enemies that mark me as his slave.

18 Dear brothers, may the grace of our Lord Jesus Christ be with you all.

Sincerely,
Paul

Ephesians

CHAPTER 1

Dear Christian friends at Ephesus, ever loyal to the Lord: This is Paul writing to you, chosen by God to be Jesus Christ's messenger.

2 May His blessings and peace be yours, sent to you from God our Father and Jesus Christ our Lord.

3 How we praise God, the Father of our Lord Jesus Christ, Who has blessed us with every blessing in heaven because we belong to Christ.

4 Long ago before He made the world God chose us to be His very own, through what Christ would do for us; He decided then to make us holy in His eyes, without a single fault—we who stand before Him covered with His love.

5 His unchanging plan has always been to adopt us into His own family by sending Jesus Christ to die for us. And He did this because He wanted to!

6 Now all praise to God for His wonderful kindness to us and His favor that He has poured out upon us, because we belong to His dearly loved Son.

7 So overflowing is His kindness towards us that He took away all our sins through the blood of His Son, by Whom we are saved;

8 And He has showered down upon us the richness

of His grace—for how well He understands us and knows what is best for us at all times.

9 God has told us His secret reason for sending Christ, a plan He decided on in mercy long ago:

10 And this was His purpose: that when the time is ripe He will gather us all together from wherever we are—in heaven or on earth—to be with Him—in Christ —forever.

11 Moreover, because of what Christ has done we have become gifts to God that He delights in, for as part of God's sovereign plan we were chosen from the beginning to be His, and all things happen just as He decided long ago.

12 God's purpose in this was that we should praise God and give glory to Him for doing these mighty things for us, who were the first to trust in Christ.

13 And because of what Christ did, all you others too, who heard the Good News about how to be saved, and trusted Christ, were marked as belonging to Christ by the Holy Spirit, Who long ago had been promised to all of us Christians.

14 His presence within us is God's guarantee that He really will give us all that He promised; and the Spirit's seal upon us means that God has already purchased us and that He guarantees to bring us to Himself. This is just one more reason for us to praise our glorious God.

15 That is why, ever since I heard of your strong faith in the Lord Jesus and of the love you have for Christians everywhere,

16, 17 I have never stopped thanking God for you.

I pray for you constantly, asking God the glorious Father of our Lord Jesus Christ to give you wisdom to see clearly and really understand who Christ is and all He has done.

18 I pray that your hearts will be flooded with light so that you can see something of the future He has called you to share. I want you to realize that God has been made rich because we who are Christ's have been given to Him!

19 I pray that you will begin to understand how incredibly great His power is to help those who believe Him. It is that same mighty power

20 That raised Christ from the dead and seated Him in the place of honor at God's right hand in heaven,

21 Far, far above any other king or ruler or dictator or leader. Yes, His honor is far more glorious than that of any one else either in this world or in the world to come.

22 And God has put all things under His feet and made Him the supreme Head of the church—

23 Which is His body, filled with Himself, the Author and Giver of everything everywhere.

CHAPTER 2

Once you were under God's curse, doomed forever for your sins.

2 You went along with the crowd and were just like all the others, full of sin, obeying Satan the mighty prince of the power of the air who is at work right now in the hearts of those who are against the Lord.

3 All of us used to be just like they are, our lives expressing the evil within us, doing every wicked thing we longed to do or thought about; we started out bad with evil natures born within us, and were under God's anger just like everyone else.

4 But God is so rich in mercy; He loved us so much

5 That even though we were spiritually dead and doomed by our sins, He gave us back our lives again when He raised Christ from the dead—only by His undeserved favor have we ever been saved—

6 And lifted us up from the grave into glory along with Christ, where we sit with Him in the heavenly realms—all because of what Christ Jesus did;

7 And now God can always point to us as examples of how very, very rich His kindness is, as shown in all He has done for us through Jesus Christ.

8 Because of His kindness you have been saved through trusting Christ. And even trusting is not of yourselves; it too is a gift from God.

9 Salvation is not a reward for the good we have done, so none of us can take any credit for it.

10 It is God Himself Who has made us what we are and given us new lives from Christ Jesus—lives which He planned out for us long ages ago to spend in helping others.

11 Never forget that once you were heathen, and that you were called godless and "unclean" by the Jews. (But their hearts too were still unclean, even though they were going through the ceremonies and rituals of the godly, for they circumcised themselves as a sign of godliness.)

12 Remember that in those days you were living utterly apart from Christ; you were enemies of God's children and He had promised you no help. You were without God, without hope.

13 But now you belong to Christ Jesus, and though you once were far away from God, now you have been brought very near to Him because of what Jesus Christ has done for you with His blood.

14 For Christ Himself is our way of peace. He has made peace between us Jews and you Gentiles by making one person out of us, breaking down the wall of anger that used to divide us.

15 By his death He ended the angry resentment between us, caused by the Jewish laws which favored the Jews and excluded the Gentiles, for He died to annul that whole system of Jewish laws. Then He took the two groups that had been opposed to each other and made them parts of Himself; thus He fused them together as one new person, and at last there was peace.

16 As parts of the same body, their anger against each other disappeared for both were reconciled to God. And so the feud ended at last at the cross.

17 And He has brought this Good News of peace to you Gentiles who were very far away from Him, and to us Jews who were near.

18 Now all of us, whether Jews or Gentiles, may come to God the Father with the Holy Spirit's help because of what Christ has done for us.

19 Now you are no longer strangers to God and foreigners to Heaven, but you are members of God's very own family, citizens of God's country, and you belong in God's household with every other Christian.

20 What a foundation you stand on now: the apostles and the prophets; and the cornerstone of the building is Jesus Christ Himself!

21 Along with Christ, we who believe are carefully joined together as parts of a beautiful, constantly growing temple for God.

22 And you also are joined in with Him and with each other by the Spirit, and are part of this dwelling place of God.

CHAPTER 3

I, Paul, the servant of Christ, am here in jail because of you—for preaching that you Gentiles are a part of God's house.

2, 3 No doubt you already know that God has given me this special work of showing God's favor to you Gentiles, as I briefly mentioned before in one of my letters. God Himself showed me this secret plan of His, that the Gentiles too are included in His kindness.

4 I say this to explain to you how I know about these things.

5 In olden times God did not share this plan with His people, but now He has revealed it by the Holy Spirit to His apostles and prophets.

6 And this is the secret: that the Gentiles will have their full share with the Jews in all the riches inherited by God's sons; they both are invited to belong to His church, and all of God's promises of mighty blessings through Christ apply to them both when they accept the Good News about Christ and what He has done for them.

7 God has given me the wonderful privilege of telling everyone about this plan of His; and He has given me His power and special ability to do it well.

8 Just think! Though I did nothing to deserve it, and though I am the most useless Christian there is, yet I was the one chosen for this special joy of telling the Gentiles the Glad News of the endless treasures available to them in Christ;

9 And to explain to everyone that God is the Saviour of the Gentiles too just as He Who made all things had secretly planned from the very beginning.

10 And His reason? To show to all the powers of heaven how perfectly wise God is when they see all of His family—Jews and Gentiles—joined together in His church,

11 Just as He had always planned to do through Jesus Christ our Lord.

12 Now we can come fearlessly right into God's presence, assured of His glad welcome when we come with Christ and trust in Him.

13 So please don't lose heart at what they are doing to me here. It is for you I am suffering and you should feel honored and encouraged.

14 When I think of the wisdom and scope of His plan I fall down on my knees and pray to the Father

15 Of all the great family of God—some of them up there in heaven and some down here on earth—

16 That out of His glorious, unlimited resources He will give you the mighty inner strengthening of His Holy Spirit.

17 And I pray that Christ will be more and more at

home in your hearts, living within you as you trust in Him. May your roots go down deep into the soil of God's marvelous love;

18, 19 And may you be able to feel and understand, as all God's children should, how long, how wide, how deep, and how high His love really is; and to experience this love for yourselves, (though it is so great that you will never see the end of it, or fully know or understand it). And so at last you will be filled up with God Himself.

20 Now glory be to God Who by His mighty power at work within us is able to do far more than we would ever dare to ask or even dream of, infinitely beyond our highest prayers, desires, thoughts, or hopes.

21 May He be given glory forever and ever through endless ages because of His master plan of salvation for the church through Jesus Christ.

CHAPTER 4

I beg you—I, a prisoner here in jail for serving the Lord—to live and act in a way worthy of those who have been chosen for such wonderful blessings as these.

2 Be humble and gentle. Be patient with each other, making allowance for each other's faults because of your love.

3 Try always to be led along together by the Holy Spirit, and so be at peace with one another.

4 We are all parts of one body, we have the same Spirit, and we have all been called to the same glorious future.

5 For us there is only one Lord, one faith, one baptism,

6 And we all have the same God and Father Who is over us all and in us all, and living through every part of us.

7 However Christ has given each of us special abilities—whatever He wants us to have out of His rich storehouse of gifts.

8 The Psalmist tells about this, for he says that when Christ returned triumphantly to heaven after His resurrection and victory over Satan, He gave generous gifts to the children of men.

9 Notice that it says He returned to heaven; this means that He had first come down from the heights of heaven, far down to the lowest parts of the earth.

10 The same One Who came down is the One Who went back up, that He might be the ruler over all things everywhere, from the farthest down to the highest up.

11 Some of us have been given special ability as apostles; to others He has given the gift of being able to preach well; some have special ability in winning people to Christ, helping them to trust Him as their Saviour; still others have a gift for caring for God's people as a shepherd does his sheep, leading and teaching them in the ways of God.

12 Why is it that He gives us these special abilities to do certain things best? It is that God's people will be equipped to do better work for Him, building up the church, the body of Christ, to a position of strength and maturity;

13 Until finally we all believe alike about our salvation and about our Saviour, God's Son, and all become full-grown in the Lord. Yes, grow to the point of being filled full with Christ.

14 Then we will no longer be like children, forever changing our minds about what we believe because someone has told us something different, or has cleverly lied to us and made the lie sound like the truth.

15, 16 Instead we will lovingly follow the truth at all times—speaking truly, dealing truly, living truly† —and so become more and more in every way like Christ who is the Head of His body, the church. Under His direction the whole body is fitted together perfectly, and each part in its own special way helps the other parts, so that the whole body is healthy and growing and full of love.

17, 18 Let me say this, then, speaking for the Lord: live no longer as the unsaved do, for they are blinded and confused. Their closed hearts are full of darkness; they are far away from the life of God because they have shut their minds against Him, and they cannot understand His ways.

19 They don't care anymore about right and wrong and have given themselves over to impure ways. They stop at nothing their evil minds can think of.

20 But that isn't the way Christ taught you!

21 If you have really heard His voice and learned from Him the truths concerning Himself,

22 Then throw off your old evil nature—the old

†Amplified New Testament

you that was a partner in your evil ways—rotten through and through, full of lust and sham.

23 Now your attitudes and thoughts must all change;

24 Yes, you must be a new and different person, holy and good. Clothe yourself with this new nature.

25 Stop lying to each other; tell the truth, for we are parts of each other and when we lie to each other we are hurting ourselves.

26 If you are angry, don't sin by nursing your grudge. Don't let the sun go down with you still angry —get over it quickly;

27 For when you are angry you give a mighty foothold to the devil.

28 If anyone is stealing he must stop it and begin using those hands of his for honest work so he can give to others in need.

29 Don't use bad language. Say only what is good and helpful to those you are talking to, and what will give them a blessing.

30 Don't cause the Holy Spirit sorrow by the way you live. Remember, He is the one who marks you present on that day when salvation from sin will be complete.

31 Stop being mean, bad-tempered and angry. Quarreling, harsh words, and dislike of others should have no place in your lives.

32 Instead, be kind to each other, tender-hearted, forgiving one another, just as God has forgiven you because you belong to Christ.

CHAPTER 5

Follow God's example in everything you do just as a much loved child imitates his father.

2 Be full of love for others, following the example of Christ Who loved you and gave Himself to God as a sacrifice to take away your sins. And God was pleased, for Christ's love for you was like sweet perfume to Him.

3 Let there be no sex sin, impurity or greed among you. Let no one be able to accuse you of any such things.

4 Dirty stories, foul talk and coarse jokes—these are not for you. Instead, remind each other of God's goodness and be thankful.

5 You can be sure of this: the kingdom of Christ and of God will never belong to anyone who is impure or greedy—for a greedy person is really an idol worshiper—he loves and worships the good things of this life more than God.

6 Don't be fooled by those who try to excuse these sins, for the terrible wrath of God is upon all those who do them.

7 Don't even associate with such people.

8 For though once your heart was full of darkness, now it is full of light from the Lord, and your behavior should show it!

9 Because of this light within you, you should do only what is good and right and true.

10 Learn as you go along what pleases the Lord.

11 Take no part in the worthless pleasures of evil and darkness, but instead, rebuke and expose them.

12 It would be shameful even to mention here those pleasures of darkness which the ungodly do.

13 When you expose them, the light shines in upon their sin and shows it up, and when they see how wrong they really are, some of them may even become children of light!

14 That is why God says, in the Old Testament, "Awake, O sleeper, and rise up from the dead; and Christ shall give you light."

15, 16 So be careful how you act; these are difficult days. Don't be fools; be wise: make the most of every opportunity you have for doing good.

17 Don't act thoughtlessly, but try to find out and do whatever the Lord wants you to.

18 Don't drink too much wine, for many evils lie along that path; be filled instead with the Holy Spirit, and controlled by Him.

19 Talk with each other much about the Lord, quoting psalms and hymns and singing sacred songs and making music in your hearts to the Lord.

20 Always give thanks for everything to our God and Father in the name of our Lord Jesus Christ.

21 Honor Christ by submitting to each other.

22 You wives must submit to your husband's leadership in the same way you submit to the Lord.

23 For a husband is in charge of his wife in the same way Christ is in charge of His body the church. (He gave His very life to take care of it and be its Saviour!)

24 So you wives must willingly obey your husbands in everything, just as the church obeys Christ.

25 And you husbands, show the same kind of love to your wives as Christ showed to the church when He died for her.

26 To make her holy and clean, washed by baptism and God's word;

27 So that He could give her to Himself as a glorious church without a single spot or wrinkle or any other blemish, being holy and without a single fault.

28 That is how husbands should treat their wives, loving them as parts of themselves. For since a man and his wife are now one, a man is really doing himself a favor and loving himself when he loves his wife!

29, 30 No one hates his own body but lovingly cares for it, just as Christ cares for His body the church, of which we are parts.

31 (That the husband and wife are one body is proved by the Scripture which says, "A man must leave his father and mother when he marries, so that he can be perfectly joined to his wife, and the two shall be one.")

32 I know this is hard to understand, but it is an illustration of the way we are parts of the body of Christ.

33 So again I say, a man must love his wife as a part of himself; and the wife must see to it that she deeply respects her husband—obeying, praising and honoring him.

CHAPTER 6

Children, obey your parents for this is right.

2 Honor your father and mother. This is the first of God's Ten Commandments that ends with a promise.

3 And this is the promise: that if you honor your

father and mother, yours will be a long life, full of blessing.

4 And now a word to you parents. Don't keep on scolding and nagging your children, making them angry and resentful. But bring them up with the loving discipline the Lord Himself approves, with suggestions and godly advice.

5 Slaves, obey your masters; be eager to give them your very best. Serve them as you would Christ.

6, 7 Don't please your master when he is watching and then shirk when he isn't looking; work gladly and hard as though working for Christ, doing the will of God with all your hearts.

8 Remember, the Lord will pay you for each good thing you do, whether you are slave or free.

9 And you slave owners must treat your slaves right, just as I have told them to treat you. Don't threaten them all the time; remember, you yourselves are slaves to Christ; you have the same Master they do, and He has no favorites.

10 Last of all I want to say this: Your strength must come from the Lord's mighty power within you.

11 Put on all of God's armor so that you will be able to stand safe against the wiles of Satan.

12 For we are not fighting against people made of flesh and blood, but against persons without bodies—the evil kings of the unseen world, those mighty satanic beings and great evil princes of darkness who rule this world; and against huge numbers of wicked spirits in the spirit world.

13 So use every piece of God's armor to resist the

enemy whenever he attacks, and when it is all over, you will still be standing up.

14 But to do this, you will need the strong belt of truth and the breastplate of God's approval.

15 Wear shoes that are able to speed you on as you preach the Good News of peace with God.

16 In every battle you will need faith as your shield to stop the fiery arrows aimed at you by Satan,

17 And you will need the helmet of salvation and the sword of the Spirit—which is the Word of God.

18 Pray all the time. Ask God for anything in line with the Holy Spirit's wishes. Plead with Him, reminding Him of your needs, and keep praying earnestly for all Christians everywhere.

19 Pray for me too and ask God to give me the right words as I boldly tell others about the Lord, and as I tell them that His salvation is for the Gentiles too.

20 I am in chains now for preaching this message from God. But pray that I will keep on speaking out boldly for Him even here in prison, as I should.

21 Tychicus, who is a well-beloved brother and faithful helper in the Lord's work, will tell you all about how I am getting along.

22 I am sending him to you for just this purpose, that you will know how we are and be encouraged by his report.

23 May God give peace to you, my Christian brothers, and love, with faith from God the Father and the Lord Jesus Christ.

24 May God's grace and blessing be upon all who sincerely love our Lord Jesus Christ.

Paul

Philippians

CHAPTER 1

From: Paul and Timothy, slaves of Jesus Christ.

To: The pastors and deacons and all the Christians in the city of Philippi.

2 May God bless you all. Yes, I pray that God our Father and the Lord Jesus Christ will give each of you His fullest blessings, and His peace in your hearts and your lives.

3 All my prayers for you are full of praise to God!

4 When I pray for you, my heart is full of joy,

5 Because of all your wonderful help in making known the Good News about Christ from the time you first heard it until now.

6 And I am sure that God Who began the good work within you will keep right on helping you grow in His grace until His task within you is finally finished on that day when Jesus Christ returns.

7 How natural it is that I should feel as I do about you, for you have a very special place in my heart. We have shared together the blessings of God, both when I was in prison and when I was out, defending the truth and telling others about Christ.

8 Only God knows how deep is my love and longing for you—with the tenderness of Jesus Christ.

9 My prayer for you is that you will overflow more

and more with love for others, and at the same time keep on growing in spiritual knowledge and insight,

10 For I want you always to see clearly the difference between right and wrong, and to be inwardly clean, no one being able to criticize you from now until our Lord returns.

11 May you always be doing those good, kind things that go along with being a child of God, for this will bring much praise and glory to the Lord.

* * * * *

12 And I want you to know this, dear brothers: everything that has happened to me here has been a great boost in getting out the Good News concerning Christ.

13 For everyone around here, including all the soldiers over at the barracks, know my chains are simply because I am a Christian.

14 And because of the chains many of the Christians here seem to have lost their fear of chains! Somehow my patience has encouraged them and they have become more and more bold in telling others about Christ.

15 Some, of course, are preaching the Good News because they are jealous of the way God has used me. They too want reputations as fearless preachers! But others have purer motives,

16, 17 Preaching because they love me, for they know that the Lord has brought me here to use me to defend the Truth. And some preach to make me jealous, thinking that their success will add to my sorrows here in jail!

18 But no matter why they are doing it, the fact

remains that the Good News about Christ is being preached and I am glad.

19 I am going to keep on being glad, for I know that as you pray for me and as the Holy Spirit helps me this is all going to turn out for my good.

20 For I live in eager expectation and hope that I will never do anything that will cause me to be ashamed of myself; but that I will always be ready to speak out boldly for Christ while I am going through all these trials here, just as I have in the past; and that I will always be an honor to Christ, whether I live or whether I must die.

* * * * *

21 For to me living means opportunities for Christ, and dying—well, that's better yet!

22 But if living will give me more opportunities to win people to Christ, then I really don't know which is best, to live or die!

23 Sometimes I want to live and at other times I don't, for I long to go and be with Christ. How much happier for *me* than being here!

24 But the fact is that I can be of more help to *you* by staying!

25 Yes, I am needed down here and so I feel certain I will be staying on earth a little longer, to help you grow and become happy in your faith;

26 My staying will make you glad and give you reason to glorify Christ Jesus for keeping me safe, when I return to visit you again!

* * * * *

27 But whatever happens to me, remember always

to live as Christians should, so that, whether I ever see you again or not, I will keep on hearing good reports that you are standing side by side with one strong purpose—to tell the Good News

28 Fearlessly, no matter what your enemies may do. They will see this as a sign of their downfall, but for you it will be a clear sign from God that He is with you, and that He will give you eternal life with Him.

29 For to you has been given the privilege not only of trusting Him but also of suffering for Him.

30 We are in this fight together. You have seen me suffer for Him in the past; and I am still in the midst of a great and terrible struggle now, as you know so well.

CHAPTER 2

Is there any such thing as Christians cheering each other up? Do you love me enough to want to help me? Does it mean anything to you that we are brothers in the Lord, sharing the same Spirit? Are your hearts tender and sympathetic at all?

2 Then make me truly happy by loving each other and agreeing wholeheartedly with each other, working together with one heart and mind and purpose.

3 Don't be selfish; don't live to make a good impression on others. Be humble, thinking of others as better than yourself.

4 Don't just think about your own affairs, but be interested in others too and in what they are doing.

5 Try to be like Jesus Christ Who,

6 Though He was God, did not demand and cling to His rights as God,

7 But laid aside His mighty power and glory, taking the disguise of a slave and becoming like men.†

8 And he humbled Himself even further, going so far as to actually die a criminal's death on a cross.

9 Yet it was because of this that God raised Him up to the heights of heaven and gave Him a Name which is above every other name,

10 That at the Name of Jesus every knee shall bow in heaven and on earth and under the earth,

11 And every tongue shall confess that Jesus Christ is Lord, to the glory of God the Father.

* * * * *

12 Dearest friends, when I was there with you, you were always so careful to follow my instructions. And now that I am away you must be even more careful to do the good things that result from being saved, obeying God with deep reverence, shrinking back from all that might displease Him.

13 For God is at work within you, helping you want to obey Him, and then helping you do what He wants.

14 In everything you do, stay away from complaining and arguing,

15 So that no one can speak a word of blame against you; you are to live clean, innocent lives as children of God in a dark world full of people who are crooked and stubborn. Shine out among them as beacon lights and

16 Hold out to them the Word of Life. Then when Christ returns how glad I will be that my work among you was so worthwhile.

† literally: "was made in the likeness of men."

17 And if my lifeblood is, so to speak, to be poured out over your faith which I am offering up to God as a sacrifice—that is, if I am to die for you—even then I will be glad, and will share my joy with each of you.
18 For you should be happy about this too and rejoice with me for having this privilege of dying for you.

* * * * *

19 I am planning, if the Lord is willing, to send Timothy to see you soon so that when he comes back he can cheer me up by telling me all about you and how you are getting along.

20 There is no one like Timothy for having a real interest in you;

21 Everyone else seems to be worrying about his own plans and not those of Jesus Christ.

22 But you know Timothy. He has been just like a son to me in helping me preach the Good News.

23 I hope to send him to you just as soon as I find out what is going to happen to me here.

24 And I am trusting the Lord that soon I myself may come to see you.

25 Meanwhile I thought I ought to send Epaphroditus back to you. You sent him to help me in my need and he and I have been real brothers, working and battling side by side.

26 Now I am sending him home again, for he has been homesick for all of you and upset because you heard that he was sick.

27 And sick he surely was; in fact he almost died. But God had mercy on him, and on me too, not allowing me to have this sorrow on top of everything else.

28 So I am all the more anxious to get him back to you again, for I know how thankful you will be to see him, and that will make me happy and lighten all my cares.

29 Welcome him in the Lord with great joy, and show your appreciation,

30 For he risked his life for the work of Christ and was at the point of death while trying to do for me the things you couldn't do because you were far away.

CHAPTER 3

Finally, dear friends, be glad in the Lord. I never get tired of telling you this and it is good for you to hear it again and again.

* * * * *

2 Watch out for those wicked men—dangerous dogs, I call them—who say you must be circumcised to be saved.

3 For it isn't the cutting of our *bodies* that makes us children of God; it is worshiping Him as we Christians do from within, with our *spirits,* that counts; that is the only true 'circumcision.' We glory in what Christ Jesus has done for us and realize that we are helpless to save ourselves.

4 Yet if anyone ever had reason to hope that he could save himself, it would be I. If others could be saved by what they are, certainly I could!

5 For I went through the Jewish initiation ceremony when I was eight days old, having been born into a pure-blooded Jewish home that was a branch of

the old original Benjamin family. So I was a real Jew if there ever was one! What's more, I was a member of the Pharisees who demand the strictest obedience to every Jewish law and custom.

6 And sincere? Yes, so much so that I greatly persecuted the church; and I tried to obey every Jewish rule and regulation right down to the very last point.

7 But all these things I once thought very worthwhile—now I've thrown them all away so that I can put my trust and hope in Christ alone.

8 Yes, everything else is worthless when compared with the priceless gain of knowing Christ Jesus my Lord. I have put aside all else, counting it worth less than nothing, in order that I can have Christ,

9 And become one with Him, no longer counting on being saved by being good enough or by obeying God's laws, but by trusting Christ to save me; for God's way of making us right with Himself depends on faith —counting on Christ alone.

10 Now I have given up everything else that I may really know Christ and experience the mighty power that brought Him back to life again, and find out what it means to suffer and die with Him,

11 So that whatever it takes I will be one who lives in the fresh newness of life of those who are alive from the dead.

12 I don't mean to say I am perfect. I haven't learned all I should even yet, but I keep working toward that day when I will finally be all that Christ saved me for and wants me to be.

13 No, dear brothers, I am still not all I should be

but I am bringing all my energies to bear on this one thing: forgetting the past and looking forward to what lies ahead,

14 I strain to reach the end of the race and receive the prize for which God is calling us up to heaven because of what Christ Jesus did for us.

* * * * *

15 I hope all of you who are mature Christians will see eye-to-eye with me on these things, and if you disagree on some points I believe that God will make it plain to you

16 If you fully obey the truth you already have.

* * * * *

17 Dear brothers, pattern your lives after mine and notice who else lives up to my example.

18 For I have told you often before, and I say it again now with tears in my eyes, there are many who walk along the Christian road who are really enemies of the cross of Christ.

19 Their future is eternal loss for their god is good food; they are proud of what they should be ashamed of; and all they think about is this life down here on earth.

20 But our homeland is that of our Saviour the Lord Jesus Christ in heaven; and we are looking forward to His return from there.

* * * * *

21 When He comes back He will take these dying bodies of ours and change them into glorious bodies like His own, using the same mighty power that He will use to conquer all else everywhere.

CHAPTER 4

Dear brother Christians, I love you and long to see you, for you are my joy and my reward for my work. My beloved friends, stay true to the Lord.

* * * * *

2 And now I want to plead with those two dear women, Euodias and Syntyche. Please, please, with the Lord's help, quarrel no more—be friends again.

3 And I ask you, my true teammate, to help these women, for they worked side by side with me in telling the Good News to others; and they worked with Clement too and the rest of my fellow workers whose names are written in the Book of Life.

* * * * *

4 Always be full of joy in the Lord; I say it again, rejoice!

5 Let everyone see that you are unselfish and gentle in all you do. Remember that the Lord is coming soon.

6 Don't worry about anything; instead, pray about everything; tell God your needs and don't forget to thank Him for His answers.

7 If you do this you will know God's peace which is far more wonderful than the human mind can understand. His peace will keep your thoughts and your hearts quiet and at rest as you trust in Christ Jesus.

* * * * *

8 And now finally, brothers, as I close this letter let me say one more thing. Fix your thoughts on what is true and good and right. Think about things that are pure and lovely, and on the fine, good things in

others. Think about all you can praise God for and be glad about.

9 Keep putting into practice all you learned from me and saw me doing, and the God of peace will be with you.

* * * * *

10 How grateful I am and how I praise the Lord because you are helping me again. I know you have always been anxious to send what you could, but for a while you didn't have the chance.

11 I'm not saying this because I was in need, for I have learned how to get along happily whether I have much or little.

12 I know how to live on almost nothing or with everything. I have learned the secret of contentment in every situation, whether it be fatness or hunger, plenty or want;

13 For I can do everything God asks me to with the help of Christ Who gives me the strength and power.

14 But even so, you have done right in helping me in my present difficulty.

15 As you well know, when I first brought the Gospel to you and then went on my way, leaving Macedonia, only you Philippians became my partners in giving and receiving. No other church did this.

16 Even when I was over in Thessalonica you sent help twice.

17 But though I appreciate your gifts, what makes me happiest is the well-earned reward you will have because of your kindness.

18 At the moment I have all I need—more than I

need! I am generously supplied with the gifts you sent me when Epaphroditus came. They are a sweet smelling sacrifice that pleases God well.

19 And it is He who will supply all your needs from His riches in glory, because of what Christ Jesus has done for us.

20 Now unto God our Father be glory forever and ever. Amen.

Sincerely,
Paul

P.S.

21 Say "hello" for me to all the Christians there; the brothers with me send their greetings too.

22 And all the other Christians here want to be remembered to you, especially those who work in Caesar's palace.

23 The blessings of our Lord Jesus Christ be upon your spirits.

Colossians

CHAPTER 1

From: Paul, chosen by God to be Jesus Christ's messenger, and from Brother Timothy.

2 *To:* the faithful Christian brothers—God's people—in the city of Colosse.

May God our Father fill you with blessings and with His great peace.

3 Whenever we pray for you we always begin by giving thanks to God the Father of our Lord Jesus Christ,

4 For we have heard how much you trust the Lord, and how much you love His people.

5 And you are looking forward to the joys of heaven, and have been ever since the Gospel first was preached to you.

6 The same Good News that came to you is going out all over the world and changing lives everywhere, just as it changed yours that very first day you heard it and understood about God's great kindness to sinners.

7 Epaphras our much-loved fellow worker was the one who brought you this Good News. He is Jesus Christ's slave, here in your place to help us.

8 And he is the one who has told us about the great

love for others which the Holy Spirit has given you.

9 So ever since we first heard about you we have kept on praying and asking God to help you understand what He wants you to do, and to make you wise about spiritual things,

10 That the way you live will always please the Lord and honor Him, that you will always be doing good, kind things for others, all the time learning to know God better and better.

11 We are praying too that you will be filled up with His mighty, glorious strength so that you can keep going no matter what happens—always full of the joy of the Lord,

12 And always thankful to the Father Who has made us fit to share all the wonderful things that belong to those who live in the kingdom of light.

13 For He has rescued us out of the darkness and gloom of Satan's kingdom and brought us into the kingdom of His dear Son

14 Who bought our freedom with His blood and forgave us all our sins.

* * * * *

15 Christ is the exact likeness of the unseen God. Now God did not create this Son of His, for He existed before God made anything at all.

16 And Christ Himself is the Creator Who made everything in heaven and earth, the things we can see and the things we can't; the spirit world with its kings and kingdoms, its rulers and authorities: all were made by Christ for His own use and glory.

17 He was before all else began and it is His power that holds everything together.

18 He is the Head of the body made up of His people—that is, His church—which He began; and He is the Leader of all who arise from the dead,† so that He is first in everything;

19 For God wanted all of Himself to be in His Son.

20 It was through what His Son did that God cleared a path for everything to come to Him, all things in heaven and on earth, for Christ's death on the cross has made peace with God for all by His blood;

21 And for you, for you were once far away from God. You were His enemies and hated Him and were separated from Him by your evil thoughts and actions, yet now He has brought you back as His friends.

22 He has done this through the death on the cross of His own human body, and now as a result Christ has brought you into the very presence of God, and you are standing there before Him with nothing left against you—nothing left that He could even chide you for;

23 That is, if you fully believe the Truth, standing in it steadfast and firm, strong in the Lord, convinced of the Good News that Jesus died for you, and never shifting from trusting Him to save you. This is the wonderful news that came to each of you and is now spreading all over the world. And I, Paul, have the joy of telling it to others.

* * * * *

24 But part of my work is to suffer for you; and

† literally: "He is the Beginning, the firstborn from the dead."

I am glad, for I am helping to finish up the remainder of Christ's sufferings for His body, the church.

* * * * *

25 God has sent me to help His church and to tell His secret plan to you Gentiles.

26, 27 For He has had a secret for centuries and generations past, but now at last it has pleased Him to tell it to those who love Him and live for Him, and the riches and glory of His plan are for you Gentiles too, and this is the secret: *that Christ in your hearts is your only hope of glory.*

28 And so everywhere we go and to all who will listen we preach Christ; warning them and teaching them as well as we know how, so that we can present each one to God, perfect because of what Christ has done for each of them.

29 This is my work, and I can do it only because Christ's mighty energy is at work within me.

CHAPTER 2

I wish you could know how much I have struggled in prayer for you and for the church at Laodicea, and for my many other friends who have never known me personally.

2 This is what I have asked of God for you: that you will be encouraged and knit together by strong ties of love, and that you will have the rich experience of knowing Christ with real certainty and clear understanding. *For God's secret plan, now at last made known, is Christ Himself.*

3 In Him lie hidden all the mighty, untapped treasures of wisdom and knowledge.

4 I am saying this because I am afraid that someone may fool you with smooth talk.

5 For though I am far away from you my heart is with you, happy because you are getting along so well, happy because of your strong faith in Christ.

6 And now just as you trusted Christ to save you, trust Him too for each day's problems; live in vital union with Him.

7 Let your roots grow down into Him and draw up nourishment from Him. See that you go on growing in the Lord, and become strong and vigorous in the truth. Let your lives overflow with joy and thanksgiving for all He has done.

8 Don't let others spoil your faith and joy with their philosophies, their wrong and shallow answers built on men's thoughts and ideas, instead of on what Christ has said.

9 For in Christ there is all of God in a human body;

10 *So you have everything when you have Christ,* and you are filled with God through your union with Christ. He is the highest ruler over every other power.

* * * * *

11 When you came to Christ He set you free from your evil desires, not by a bodily operation of circumcision but by a spiritual operation, the baptism of your souls.

12 For in baptism you see how your old, evil nature died with Him and was buried with Him; and then you came up out of death with Him into a new life be-

cause you trusted the Word of the mighty God Who raised Christ from the dead.

13 You were dead in sins, and your sinful desires were not yet cut away. Then He gave you a share in the very life of Christ, for He forgave all your sins,

14 And blotted out the charges proved against you, the list of His commandments which you had not obeyed. He took this list of sins and destroyed it by nailing it to Christ's cross.

15 In this way God took away Satan's power to accuse you of sin, and God openly displayed to the whole world Christ's triumph at the cross where your sins were all taken away.

16 So don't let anyone criticize you for what you eat or drink, or for not celebrating Jewish holidays and feasts or new moon ceremonies or Sabbaths.

17 For these were only temporary rules that ended when Christ came. They were only shadows of the real thing—of Christ Himself.

18 Don't let anyone declare you lost when you refuse to worship angels, as they say you must. They have seen a vision, they say, and know you should. These proud men have a very clever imagination.

19 But they are not connected to Christ, the Head to which all of us who are His body are joined; for we are joined together by His strong sinews and we grow only as we get our nourishment and strength from Him.

20 Since you died, as it were, with Christ and this has set you free from following the world's idea of being saved by certain rules such as what you eat or

drink, why do you keep right on following it anyway, still bound by such rules as

21 Not eating, tasting, or even touching certain foods?

22 Such rules are mere human teachings, for food was made to be eaten and used up.

23 These rules may seem good, for rules of this kind require strong devotion and are humiliating and hard on the body, but they have no effect when it comes to conquering a person's evil thoughts and desires. They only make him proud.

CHAPTER 3

Since you became alive again, so to speak, when Christ arose from the dead, now set your sights on the rich treasures and joys awaiting you in heaven where Christ sits beside God in the place of honor and power.

2 Let heaven fill your thoughts; don't spend your time worrying about things down here.

3 You should have as little desire for this world as a dead person does. Your real life is in heaven with Christ and God.

4 And when Christ Who is our real life comes back again, then you will shine with Him, and share in all His glories.

5 Away then with sinful, earthly things; deaden the evil desires lurking within you; have nothing to do with sexual sin, impurity, lust and shameful desires; don't worship the good things of this life, for that is idolatry.

6 God's terrible anger is upon those who do such things.

7 You used to do them when your life was still part of this world;

8 But now is the time to cast off and throw away all these rotten garments of anger, hatred, cursing and dirty language.

9 Don't tell lies to each other; it was your old life with all its wickedness that did that sort of thing; now it is dead and gone.

10 You are living a brand new kind of life that is ever learning more and more of what is right, and trying to be more and more like Christ Who created this new life within you.

11 In this new life one's nationality or race or education or social position is unimportant. Such things mean nothing; whether a person has Christ is what matters, and He is equally available to all.

12 Since you have been chosen by God Who has given you a new kind of life, and because of His deep love and concern for you, you should practice tender-hearted pity and kindness to others. Don't worry about making a good impression on them but be ready to suffer quietly and patiently.

13 Be gentle and ready to forgive; never hold grudges. Remember, the Lord forgave you, so you must forgive others.

14 Most of all, let love guide your life for then the whole church will stay together in perfect harmony.

15 Let the peace of heart which comes from Christ be always present in your hearts and lives, for this is

your responsibility and privilege as members of His body. And always be thankful.

16 Remember what Christ taught and let His words enrich your lives and make you wise; teach them to each other and sing them out in psalms and hymns and spiritual songs, singing to the Lord with thankful hearts.

17 And whatever you do or say, let it be as a representative of the Lord Jesus, and come with Him into the presence of God the Father to give Him your thanks.

18 You wives, submit yourselves to your husbands, for that is what the Lord has planned for you.

19 And you husbands must be loving and kind to your wives and not bitter against them, nor harsh.

20 You children must always obey your fathers and mothers, for that pleases the Lord.

21 Fathers, don't scold your children so much that they become discouraged and quit trying.

22 You slaves must always obey your earthly masters, not only trying to please them when they are watching you but all the time; obey them willingly because of your love for the Lord and because you want to please Him.

23 Work hard and cheerfully at all you do, just as though you were working for the Lord and not merely for your masters,

24 Remembering that it is the Lord Christ Who is going to pay you, giving you your full portion of all He owns. He is the One you are really working for.

25 And if you don't do your best for Him, He will pay you in a way that you won't like—for He has no special favorites who can get away with shirking.

CHAPTER 4

You slave owners must be just and fair to all your slaves. Always remember that you too have a Master up in heaven Who is closely watching you.

* * * * *

2 Don't be weary in prayer; keep at it; watch for God's answers and remember to be thankful when they come.

3 Don't forget to pray for us too, that God will give us many chances to preach the Good News of Christ for which I am here in jail.

4 Pray that I will be bold enough to tell it freely and fully, and make it plain, as of course I should.

5 Make the most of your chances to tell others the Good News. Be wise in all your contacts with them.

6 Let your conversation be gracious as well as sensible, for then you will have the right answer for everyone.

* * * * *

7 Tychicus our much loved brother will tell you how I am getting along. He is a hard worker and serves the Lord with me.

8 I have sent him on this special trip just to see how you are, and to comfort and encourage you.

9 I am also sending Onesimus, a faithful and much loved brother who is one of your own people. He and Tychicus will give you all the latest news.

10 Aristarchus who is with me here as a prisoner sends you his love, and so does Mark, a relative of

Barnabas. As I said before, give him a hearty welcome if he comes to you.

11 Jesus Justus also sends his love. These are the only Jewish Christians working with me here, and what a comfort they have been!

12 Epaphras, from your city, a servant of Christ Jesus, sends you his love. He is always earnestly praying for you, asking God to make you strong and perfect and to help you know His will in everything you do.

13 I can assure you that he has worked hard for you with his prayers, and also for the Christians in Laodicea and Hierapolis.

14 Dear doctor Luke sends his love, and so does Demas.

15 Please give my greeting to the Christian friends at Laodicea, and to Nymphas, and to those who meet in his home.

16 By the way, after you have read this letter will you pass it on to the church at Laodicea? And read the letter I wrote to them.

17 And say to Archippus, "Be sure that you do all the Lord has told you to."

18 Here is my own greeting in my own handwriting: Remember me here in jail. May God's blessings surround you.

Paul

I Thessalonians

CHAPTER 1

From: Paul, Silas and Timothy.

To: The Church at Thessalonica—to you who belong to God the Father and the Lord Jesus Christ: May blessing and peace of heart be your rich gifts from God our Father, and from Jesus Christ our Lord.

2 We always thank God for you and pray for you constantly.

3 We never forget your loving deeds as we talk to our God and Father about you, and your strong faith and steady looking forward to the return of our Lord Jesus Christ.

4 We know that God has chosen you, dear brothers, much beloved of God.

5 For when we brought you the Good News, it was not just meaningless chatter to you, but you listened with great interest. What we told you produced a powerful effect upon you, for the Holy Spirit gave you great and full assurance that what we said was true. And you know how our very lives were further proof to you of the truth of our message.

6 So you became our followers and the Lord's; for you received our messages with joy from the Holy Spirit in spite of the trials and sorrows it brought you.

7 Then you yourselves became an example to all the other Christians in Macedonia and Achaia.

8 And now the Word of the Lord has spread out from you to others everywhere, not only to those in Macedonia and Achaia, for wherever we go we find people telling us about your remarkable faith in God. We don't need to tell *them* about it,

9 For *they* keep telling *us* about the wonderful welcome you gave us, and how you turned away from your idols to God so that now the living and true God only is your master.

10 And they speak of how you are looking forward to the return of God's Son from heaven—Jesus, Whom God brought back to life—and He is our only Saviour from God's terrible anger against sin.

CHAPTER 2

You yourselves know, dear brothers, how worthwhile that visit was.

2 You know how badly we had been treated at Philippi just before we came to you, and how much we suffered there. Yet God gave us the courage to boldly repeat the same message to you, even though we were surrounded by enemies.

3 So you can see that we were not preaching with any false motives or evil purposes in mind; we were perfectly straightforward and sincere.

4 For we speak as messengers from God, trusted by Him to tell the truth; we change His message not one whit to suit the taste of those who hear it; for we

serve God alone, Who examines our hearts' deepest thoughts.

5 Never once did we try to win you with flattery, as you very well know, and God knows we were not just pretending to be your friends so that you would give us money!

6 As for praise, we have never asked for it from you or anyone else, although as apostles of Christ we certainly had a right to some honor from you.

7 But we were as gentle among you as a mother feeding and caring for her own children.

8 We loved you dearly—so dearly that we gave you not only God's message, but our own lives too.

9 Don't you remember, dear brothers, how hard we worked among you? Night and day we toiled and sweated to earn enough to live on so that our expenses would not be a burden to anyone there, as we preached God's Good News among you.

10 You yourselves are our witnesses—as is God—that we have been pure and honest and faultless toward every one of you.

11 We talked to you as a father to his own children—don't you remember?—pleading with you, encouraging you and even demanding

12 That your daily lives should not embarrass God, but bring joy to Him Who invited you into His kingdom and into His glory.

13 And we will never stop thanking God for this: that when we preached to you, you didn't think of the words we spoke as being just our own, but you accepted what we said as the very Word of God—which of course

it was and it changed your lives when you believed it.

14 And then, dear brothers, you suffered what the churches in Judea did, persecution from your own countrymen, just as they suffered from their own people the Jews.

15 They killed the Lord Jesus and even their own prophets, and have brutally persecuted us and driven us out. They are against both God and man,

16 Trying to keep us from preaching to the Gentiles for fear some might be saved; and so their sins continue to grow. But the anger of God has caught up with them at last.

17 Dear brothers, after we left you and had been away from you but a very little while, (though our hearts never left you), we tried hard to come back again to see you once more.

18 We wanted very much to come and I, Paul, tried again and again, but Satan stopped us.

19 For what is it we live for, that gives us hope and joy and is our proud reward and crown? It is you! Yes, you will bring us much joy as we stand together before our Lord Jesus Christ when He comes back again.

20 For you are our glory and joy.

CHAPTER 3

Finally when I could stand it no longer I decided to stay alone in Athens

2, 3 And send Timothy, our brother and fellow worker, God's minister, to visit you to strengthen your faith and encourage you, lest you become fainthearted in all the troubles you were going through; (though as you know such troubles are a part of God's plan for us Christians.

4 Even while we were still with you we warned you ahead of time that suffering would soon come—and it did.)

5 When I could bear the suspense no longer I sent Timothy to find out whether your faith was still strong. I was afraid that perhaps Satan had gotten the best of you and that all our work had been useless.

6 And now Timothy has just returned and brings the welcome news that your faith and love are as strong as ever, and that you remember our visit with joy and want to see us just as much as we want to see you.

7 So we are greatly comforted, dear brothers, in all of our own crushing troubles and suffering here, now that we know you are standing true to the Lord.

8 We can bear anything as long as we know that you remain strong in Him.

9 How can we thank God enough for you and for all the joy and delight you have given us in our praying for you?

10 For night and day we pray on and on for you, asking God to let us see you again, to fill up any little cracks there may yet be in your faith.

11 May God our Father Himself and our Lord Jesus send us back to you again.

12 And may the Lord make your love grow and overflow to each other and everyone else, just as our love does to you;

13 And so God our Father will make your hearts strong, sinless and holy as you stand before Him, when

our Lord Jesus Christ returns with all who belong to Him.

CHAPTER 4

Let me add this, dear brothers: you already know how to please God in your daily living, for you know the commands we gave you from the Lord Jesus Himself. Now we beg you—yes, we demand of you in the name of the Lord Jesus—that you live more and more closely to that ideal.

3, 4 For God wants you to be holy and pure, and to keep clear of all sex sin so that each of you will marry in holiness and honor—

5 Not in lustful passion as the heathen do, in their ignorance of God and His ways.

6 And this also is God's will: that you never cheat in this matter by taking another man's wife, because the Lord will pay you back terribly for this, as we have solemnly told you before.

7 For God has not called us to be dirty minded and full of lust, but to be holy and clean.

8 If anyone refuses to live by these rules he is not disobeying the rules of men but of God Who gives His *Holy* Spirit to you.

9 But what of the pure brotherly love there is among God's people? Well, I don't need to say very much about that I feel sure! For God Himself is teaching you to love one another.

10 Indeed, your love is strong for all the brethren throughout your whole nation. Even so, dear friends, we beg you to love them more and more.

11 This should be your ambition—to live a quiet life, minding your own business and doing your own work, just as we told you before.

12 As a result people who are not Christians will trust and respect you, and you will not need to depend on others for enough money to pay your bills.

* * * * *

13 And now, dear brothers, I want you to know what happens to a Christian when he dies so that you will not be full of sorrow when it happens, like those who have no hope.

14 For since we believe that Jesus died and then came back to life again, we can also believe that when Jesus returns, God will bring back with Him all the Christians who have died.

15 I can tell you this, direct from the Lord, that we who are still living when the Lord returns will not rise to meet Him ahead of those who are in their graves.

16 For the Lord Himself will come down from heaven with a mighty shout and with the soul-stirring cry of the archangel and the great trumpet-call of God. And the Christians who are dead will be the first to rise to meet the Lord.

17 Then we who are still alive and remain on the earth will catch up to them in the clouds to meet the Lord in the air and remain with Him forever.

18 So comfort each other with this news.

CHAPTER 5

When is all this going to happen? I really don't need to say anything about that, dear brothers,

2 For you know perfectly well that no one knows; for that day of the Lord will come unexpectedly like a thief in the night.

3 When people are saying, "All is well, everything is quiet and peaceful"—then all of a sudden disaster will fall upon them as suddenly as a woman's birth pains when her child is born. And these people will not be able to get away anywhere—there will be no place to hide.

4 But dear brothers, you are not in the dark about these things, and you won't be surprised as by a thief when that day of the Lord comes.

5 For you are all children of the light and of the day, and do not belong to darkness and night.

6 Be on your guard, not asleep like the others. Watch for His return and stay sober.

7 Night is the time for sleep and the time when people get drunk.

8 But let us who live in the light keep sober, protected by the armor of faith and love, and wearing as our helmet the happy hope of salvation.

9 For God has not chosen to pour out His anger upon us, but to save us through our Lord Jesus Christ;

10 He died for us so that we can live with Him forever, whether we are dead or alive at the time of His return.

11 So encourage each other and build each other up, just as you are already doing.

12 Dear brothers, honor the officers of your church who work hard among you and warn you against all that is wrong.

13 Think highly of them and give them your wholehearted love because of their work. And remember, "no quarreling" among yourselves.

14 Dear brothers, warn those who are lazy or wild; comfort those who are frightened; take tender care of those who are weak; and be patient with everyone.

15 See that no one pays back evil for evil, but always try to do good to each other and to everyone else.

16 Always be joyful.

17 Always keep on praying.

18 Always be thankful no matter what happens, for that is God's will for you who belong to Christ Jesus.

19 Do not smother the Holy Spirit.

20 Do not scoff at those who prophesy,

21 But test all things to see if they are true, and if they are, hold on to them.

22 Keep away from every kind of evil.

23 May the God of peace Himself make you entirely clean; and may your spirit and soul and body be kept strong and blameless until that day when our Lord Jesus Christ comes back again.

24 God Who called you to become His child will do all this for you, just as He promised.

25 Dear brothers, pray for us.

26 Shake hands for me with all the brothers there.

27 I command you in the name of the Lord to read this letter to all the Christians.

28 And may rich blessings from our Lord Jesus Christ be with you, every one.

Sincerely,
Paul

II Thessalonians

CHAPTER 1

From: Paul, Silas and Timothy.

To: The church of Thessalonica—kept safe in God our Father and in the Lord Jesus Christ.

2 May God the Father and the Lord Jesus Christ give you rich blessings, and peaceful hearts and minds.

3 Dear brothers, giving thanks to God for you is not only the right thing to do, but is our duty to God, because of the really wonderful way your faith has grown, and because of your growing love for each other.

4 We are happy to tell other churches about your patience and complete faith in God, in spite of all the crushing troubles and hardships you are going through.

5 This is just one example of the fair, just way God does things, for He is using your sufferings to make you ready for His kingdom,

6 While at the same time He is preparing judgment and punishment for those who are hurting you.

7 And so I would say to you who are suffering, God will give you rest along with us when the Lord Jesus appears suddenly from heaven in flaming fire with His mighty angels,

8 Bringing judgment on those who do not wish to know God, and who refuse to submit to His plan to save them through our Lord Jesus Christ.

9 They will be punished in everlasting hell, forever shut away from the face of the Lord, never to see the glory of His power

10 When He comes to receive glory and wonder and admiration for all He has done for His people, His saints. And you will be with Him, because you have believed God's word which we gave you.

11 And so we keep on praying for you that our God will make you the kind of children He wants to have—will make you as good as you wish you could be!—rewarding your faith with His power.

12 Then everyone will give glory to the Name of the Lord Jesus Christ because of the results they see in you, and your great glory will be that you belong to Him. For that is the way God and the Lord Jesus Christ have planned it.

CHAPTER 2

And now, what about the coming again of our Lord Jesus Christ, and our being gathered together to meet Him? Please don't be upset and excited, dear brothers, by the rumor that this day of the Lord has already begun. If you hear of people having visions and special messages from God about this, or letters that are supposed to have come from me, don't believe them.

3 Don't be carried away and deceived regardless of what they say. For that day will not come until two things happen: first, there will be a time of great rebellion against God, and then the man of rebellion will come—the son of hell.

4 He will defy every god there is, and tear down

every other object of adoration and worship. He will go in and sit as God in the temple of God, claiming that he is God Himself.

5 Don't you remember that I told you this when I was with you?

6 And you know Who is keeping him from being here already; for he can come only when his time is ready.

7 As for the work this man of rebellion and hell will do when he comes, it is already going on, but he himself will not come until the One Who is holding him back steps out of the way.

8 And then this wicked one will appear, whom the Lord Jesus will burn up with the breath of His mouth and destroy by His presence when He returns.

9 This man of sin will come as Satan's tool, full of Satanic power, and will trick everyone with strange sights, and will pretend to do great miracles.

10 He will completely fool those who are on their way to hell because they have said "no" to the Truth; they have refused to believe it and love it, or let it save them.

11 So God will allow them to believe these lies with all their hearts,

12 And all of them will be justly judged for believing falsehood, refusing the Truth, and enjoying their sins.

13 But we must forever give thanks to God for you, our brothers loved by the Lord, because God chose from the very first to give you salvation, cleansing you by the work of the Holy Spirit and by your trusting in the Truth.

14 Through us He told you the Good News. Through us He called you to share in the glory of our Lord Jesus Christ.

15 With all these things in mind, dear brothers, stand firm and keep a strong grip on the truth that we taught you in our letters and during the time we were with you.

16 May our Lord Jesus Christ Himself and God our Father, Who has loved us and given us everlasting comfort and hope which we don't deserve,

17 Comfort your hearts with all comfort, and help you in every good thing you say and do.

CHAPTER 3

Finally, dear brothers, as I come to the end of this letter I ask you to pray for us. Pray first that the Lord's message will spread rapidly and triumph wherever it goes, winning converts everywhere as it did when it came to you.

2 Pray too that we will be saved out of the clutches of evil men, for not everyone loves the Lord.

3 But the Lord is faithful; He will make you strong and guard you from Satanic attacks of every kind.

4 And we trust the Lord that you are putting into practice the things we taught you, and that you always will.

5 May the Lord bring you ever deeper into an understanding of the love of God and of the patience that comes from Christ.

6 Now here is a command, dear brothers, given in

the name of our Lord Jesus Christ by His authority: stay away from any Christian who spends his days in laziness and does not follow the ideal of hard work we set up for you.

7 For you well know that you ought to follow our example: you never saw us loafing;

8 We never accepted food from anyone without buying it; we worked hard day and night for the money we needed to live on, in order that we would not be a burden to any of you.

9 It wasn't that we didn't have the right to ask you to feed us, but we wanted to show you, firsthand, how you should work for your living.

10 Even while we were still there with you we gave you this rule: "He who does not work shall not eat."

11 Yet we hear that some of you are living in laziness, refusing to work, and wasting your time in gossiping.

12 In the name of the Lord Jesus Christ we appeal to such people—we command them—to quiet down, get to work, and earn their own living.

13 And to the rest of you I say, dear brothers, never be tired of doing right.

14 If anyone refuses to obey what we say in this letter, notice who he is and stay away from him, that he may be ashamed of himself.

15 Don't think of him as an enemy, but speak to him as you would to a brother who needs to be warned.

16 May the Lord of peace Himself give you His peace no matter what happens. The Lord be with you all.

17 Now here is my greeting which I am writing with my own hand, as I do at the end of all my letters, for proof that it really is from me. This is in my own handwriting.

18 May the blessing of our Lord Jesus Christ be upon you all.

Sincerely,
Paul

I Timothy

CHAPTER 1

From: Paul, a missionary of Jesus Christ, sent out by God our Saviour and by Jesus Christ our Lord—our only hope.

2 *To:* Timothy.

Timothy, you are like a son to me in the things of the Lord. May God our Father and Jesus Christ our Lord show you His kindness and mercy and give you great peace of heart and mind.

3, 4 As I said when I left for Macedonia, please stay there in Ephesus and try to stop the men who are teaching such wrong doctrine. Put an end to their myths and fables, and their idea of being saved by finding favor with an endless chain of angels leading up to God —wild ideas that stir up questions and arguments instead of helping people accept God's plan of faith.

5 What I am eager for is that all the Christians there will be filled with love that comes from pure hearts, and that their minds will be clean and their faith strong.

6 But these teachers have missed this whole idea and spend their time arguing and talking foolishness.

7 They want to become famous as teachers of the laws of Moses when they haven't the slightest idea what those laws really show us.

8 Those laws are good when used as God intended,

9 But they were not made for us, whom God has saved; they are for sinners who hate God, have rebellious hearts, curse and swear, attack their fathers and mothers, and murder.

10, 11 Yes, these laws are made to show up the sin of those who are immoral and impure; for homosexuals, kidnappers and liars and anyone else who does anything that contradicts the glorious Gospel of our blessed God, Whose messenger I am.

12 How thankful I am to Christ Jesus our Lord for choosing me as one of His messengers, and giving me the strength to be faithful to Him,

13 Even though I used to scoff at the name of Christ. I hunted down His people, harming them in every way I could. But God had mercy on me because I didn't know what I was doing, for I didn't know Christ at that time.

14 Oh how kind our Lord was, for He showed me how to trust Him and become full of the love of Christ Jesus.

15 How true it is, and how I long that everyone should know it, that Christ Jesus came into the world to save sinners—and I was the greatest of them all.

16 But God had mercy on me so that Christ Jesus could use me as an example to show everyone how patient He is with even the worst sinners, so that others will realize that they too can have everlasting life.

17 Glory and honor to God for ever and ever. He is the King of the ages, the unseen One Who never dies; He alone is God, and full of wisdom. Amen.

18 Now Timothy, my son, here is my command

to you: fight well in the Lord's battles, just as the Lord told us you would through His prophets.

19 Cling tightly to your faith in Christ and always keep your conscience clear, doing what you know is right. For some people have disobeyed their consciences and have deliberately done what they knew was wrong. It isn't surprising that soon they lost their faith in Christ after defying God like that.

20 Hymenaeus and Alexander are two examples of this. I had to give them over to Satan to punish them until they could learn not to bring shame to the Name of Christ.

CHAPTER 2

Here are my directions: pray much for others; plead for God's mercy upon them; give thanks for all He is going to do for them.

2 Pray in this way for kings and all others who are in authority over us, or are in places of high responsibility, so that we can live in peace and quietness, spending our time doing good and thinking much about the Lord.

3 This is good and pleases God our Saviour,

4 For He longs for all to be saved and to understand this truth:

5 That God is on one side and all the people on the other side, and Christ Jesus, Himself man, is between them to bring them together,

6 By giving His life for all mankind. This is the message which at the proper time God gave to the world.

7 And I have been chosen—this is the absolute truth—as God's minister and missionary to teach this truth to the Gentiles, and to show them God's plan of salvation through faith.

8 So I want men everywhere to pray with holy hands lifted up to God, free from sin and anger and resentment.

9, 10 And the women should be the same way, quiet and sensible in manner and clothing. Christian women should be noticed for being kind and good, not for the way they fix their hair or because of their jewels or fancy clothes.

11 Women should listen and learn quietly and humbly.

12 I never let women teach men or lord it over them. Let them be silent in your church meetings.

13 Why? Because God made Adam first, and afterwards He made Eve.

14 And Adam was not fooled by Satan, but Eve was, and sinned as a result.

15 So God sent pain and sorrow to women when their children are born, but He will save their souls if they trust in Him, living quiet, good and loving lives.

CHAPTER 3

It is a true saying that if a man wants to be a pastor,† he has a good ambition.

2 For a pastor must be a good man whose life can-

†more literally, "elder" (as in Titus 1:5, 7). So also throughout I Timothy.

not be spoken against. He must have only one wife, and he must be hard-working and thoughtful, orderly, and full of good deeds. He must enjoy having guests in his home, and must be a good Bible teacher.

3 He must not be a drinker or quarrelsome, but he must be gentle and kind, and not be one who loves money.

4 He must have a well-behaved family, with children who obey quickly and quietly.

5 For if a man can't make his own little family behave, how can he help the whole church?

6 The pastor must not be a new Christian, because he might be proud of being chosen so soon, and pride comes before a fall. (Satan's downfall is an example.)

7 Also he must be well spoken of by people outside the church, those who aren't Christians, so that Satan can't trap him with many accusations, and leave him without freedom to lead his flock.

8 The deacons must be the same sort of good, steady men as the pastors. They must not be heavy drinkers and must not be greedy for money.

9 They must be earnest, wholehearted followers of Christ Who is the hidden source of their faith.

10 Before they are asked to be deacons they should be given other jobs in the church as a test of their character and ability, and if they do well, then they may be chosen as deacons.

11 Their wives must be thoughtful, not heavy drinkers, not gossipers, but faithful in all they do.

12 Deacons should have only one wife and they should have happy, obedient families.

13 Those who do well as deacons will be well rewarded both by respect from others and also by developing their own confidence and bold trust in the Lord.

14 I am writing these things to you now, even though I hope to be with you soon,

15 So that if I don't come for awhile you will know what kind of men you should choose as officers for the church of the living God, which contains and holds high the truth of God.

16 It is quite true that the way to live a godly life is not an easy matter. But the answer lies in Christ, Who came to earth as a man, was proved spotless and pure in His Spirit, was served by angels, was preached among the nations, was accepted by men everywhere and was received up again to His glory in heaven.

CHAPTER 4

But the Holy Spirit tells us clearly that in the last times some in the church will turn away from Christ and become eager followers of teachers with devilish ideas.

2 These teachers will tell lies with straight faces and do it so often that their consciences won't even bother them.

3 They will say it is wrong to be married and wrong to eat meat, even though God gave these things to well-taught Christians to enjoy and be thankful for.

4 For everything God made is good, and we may eat it gladly if we are thankful for it,

5 And if we ask God to bless it, for it is made good by the Word of God and prayer.

6 If you explain this to the others you will be doing

your duty as a worthy pastor who is fed by faith and by the true teaching you have followed.

7 Don't waste time arguing over foolish ideas and silly myths and legends. Spend your time and energy in the exercise of keeping spiritually fit.

8 Bodily exercise is all right, but spiritual exercise is much more important and is a tonic for all you do. So exercise yourself spiritually and practice being a better Christian, because that will help you not only now in this life, but in the next life too.

9, 10 This is the truth and everyone should accept it. We work hard and suffer much in order that people will believe it, for our hope is in the living God Who died for all, and particularly for those who have accepted His salvation.

11 Teach these things and make sure everyone learns them well.

12 Don't let anyone think little of you because you are young. Be their ideal; let them follow the way you teach and live; be a pattern for them in your love, your faith, and your clean thoughts.

13 Until I get there, read and explain the Scriptures to the church; preach God's word.

14 Be sure to use the abilities God gave you through His prophets when the elders of the church laid their hands upon your head.

15 Put these abilities to work; throw yourself into your tasks so that everyone may notice your improvement and progress.

16 Keep a close watch on all you do and think. Stay true to what is right and God will bless you and use you to help others.

CHAPTER 5

Never speak sharply to an older man, but plead with him respectfully just as though he were your own father. Talk to the younger men as you would to much-loved brothers.

2 Treat the older women as mothers, and the girls as your sisters, thinking only pure thoughts about them.

3 The church should take loving care of women whose husbands have died if they don't have anyone else to help them.

4 But if they have children or grandchildren, these are the ones who should take the responsibility, for kindness should begin at home, supporting needy parents. This is something that pleases God very much.

5 The church should care for widows who are poor and alone in the world if they are looking to God for His help, and spending much time in prayer;

6 But not if they are spending their time running around gossiping, seeking only pleasure and thus ruining their souls.

7 This should be your church rule so that the Christians will know and do what is right.

8 But anyone who won't care for his own relatives when they need help, especially those living in his own family, has no right to say he is a Christian. Such a person is worse than the heathen.

9 A widow who wants to become one of the special church workers should be at least sixty years old and have been married only once.

10 She must be well thought of by everyone because

of the good she has done. Has she brought up her children well? Has she been kind to strangers as well as to other Christians? Has she helped those who are sick and hurt? Is she always ready to show kindness?

11 The younger widows should not become members of this special group because after awhile they are likely to disregard their vow to Christ and marry again.

12 And so they will stand condemned because they broke their first promise.

13 Besides, they are likely to be lazy and spend their time gossiping around from house to house, getting into other people's business.

14 So I think it is better for these younger widows to marry again and have children, and take care of their own homes, then no one will be able to say anything against them.

15 For I am afraid that some of them have already turned away from the church and been led astray by Satan.

16 Let me remind you again that if you have relatives who are widows, you must take care of them. Don't leave it to the church. Then the church can spend its money keeping widows who are all alone and have nowhere else to turn.

17 Pastors who do their work well should be paid accordingly and be highly appreciated, especially those who work hard at both preaching and teaching.

18 For the Scriptures say, "Never tie up the mouth of an ox when it is treading out the grain—let him eat as he goes along!" And in another place, "Those who work deserve their pay!"

19 Don't listen to complaints against the pastor unless there are two or three witnesses to accuse him.

20 If he has really sinned, then he should be rebuked in front of the whole church so that no one else will follow his example.

21 I solemnly command you in the presence of God and the Lord Jesus Christ and the holy angels to do this whether the pastor is a special friend of yours or not. All must be treated exactly the same.

22 Never be in a hurry about choosing a pastor or you may overlook his sins and then it will look as if you approve of them. Be sure that you yourself stay away from all sin.

23 By the way, this doesn't mean you should completely give up drinking wine. You ought to take a little sometimes as medicine for your stomach because you are sick so often.

24 Remember that some men, even pastors, lead sinful lives and everyone knows it. In such situations you can do something about it. But in other cases only the judgment day will reveal the terrible truth.

25 In the same way, everyone knows how much good some pastors do, but sometimes their good deeds aren't known until long afterward.

CHAPTER 6

You Christian slaves should work hard for your owners and respect them; never let it be said that Christ's people are poor workers. Don't let the name of God and His teaching be laughed at because of you.

2 If your owner is a Christian, don't slow down just because he is your brother; work all the harder because you know that a beloved Christian is being helped by your work. Teach these truths, Timothy, and encourage all to obey them.

3 Some may deny these things, but they are the sound, wholesome teachings of the Lord Jesus Christ and are the foundation for a godly life.

4 Anyone who says anything different is both proud and stupid. He is quibbling over the meaning of Christ's words and stirring up arguments ending in jealously and anger, and that leads to name-calling and evil suspicions.

5 These men who argue, their minds warped by sin, don't know how to tell the truth; to them the Gospel is just a means of making money. Keep away from them.

6 Do you want to be truly rich? You already are if you are happy and good.

7 After all we didn't bring any money with us when we came into the world, and we can't carry away a single penny when we die.

8 So we should be well satisfied without money if we have enough food and clothing.

9 But people who long to be rich soon begin to do all kinds of wrong things to get money, things that hurt them and make them evil-minded and finally send them to hell itself.

10 For the love of money is the first step toward all kinds of sin. Some people have even turned away from God because of their love for it, and as a result have pierced themselves with many sorrows.

11 Oh Timothy, you are God's man. Run from all

these evil things and work instead at what is right and good, learning to trust Him and love others, and to be patient and gentle.

12 Fight on for God. Hold tightly to the eternal life which God has given you, and which you have confessed with such a ringing confession before many witnesses.

13 I command you before God Who gives life to all, and before Christ Jesus Who gave a fearless testimony before Pontius Pilate,

14 That you fulfill all He has told you to do, so that no one can find fault with you from now until our Lord Jesus Christ returns.

15 For in due season Christ will be revealed from heaven by the blessed and only Almighty God, the King of Kings and Lord of Lords,

16 Who alone can never die, Who lives in light so terrible that no human being can approach Him. No mere man has ever seen Him, nor ever will. Unto Him be honor and everlasting power and dominion forever and ever. Amen.

17 Tell those who are rich not to be proud and not to trust in their money which will soon be gone, but their pride and trust should be in the living God Who always richly gives us all we need for our enjoyment.

18 Tell them to use their money to do good. They should be rich in good works and should give happily to those in need, always being ready to share with others what God has given them.

19 By doing this they will be storing up real treasure for themselves in heaven—it is the only safe invest-

ment for eternity! And they will be living a fruitful Christian life down here.

20 Oh Timothy, don't fail to do these things that God entrusted to you. Keep out of foolish arguments with those who boast of their "knowledge" and thus prove their lack of it.

21 Some of these people have missed the most important thing in life—they don't know God. May God's mercy be upon you all.

Sincerely,
Paul

II Timothy

CHAPTER 1

From: Paul, Jesus Christ's missionary, sent out by God to tell men and women everywhere about the eternal life He has promised them through faith in Jesus Christ.

2 *To:* Timothy, my dear son. May God the Father and Christ Jesus our Lord shower you with His kindness, mercy and peace.

3 How I thank God for you, Timothy. I pray for you every day, and many times during the long nights I beg my God to bless you richly. He is my fathers' God, and mine, and my only purpose in life is to please Him.

4 How I long to see you again. How happy I would be, for I remember your tears as we left each other.

5 I know how much you trust the Lord, just as your mother Eunice and your grandmother Lois do; and I feel sure you are still trusting Him as much as ever.

6 This being so, I want to remind you to stir up the strength and boldness that is in you, that came upon you when I laid my hands upon your head and blessed you.

7 For the Lord does not want you to be afraid of

people, but to be wise and strong, and to love them and enjoy being with them.

8 If you will stir up this inner power, you will never be afraid to tell others about our Lord, or to let them know that I am your friend even though I am here in jail for Christ's sake. You will be ready to suffer with me for the Lord, for He will give you strength in suffering.

9 It is He Who saved us and chose us for His holy work, not because we deserved it but because that was His plan long before the world began—to show His love and kindness to us through Christ.

10 And now He has made all this plain to us by the coming of our Saviour Jesus Christ Who broke the power of death and showed us the way of everlasting life through trusting Him.

11 And God has chosen me to be His missionary, to preach to the Gentiles and teach them.

12 That is why I am suffering here in jail and I am certainly not ashamed of it, for I know the One in Whom I trust, and I am sure that He is able to safely guard all that I have given Him until the day of His return.

13 Hold tightly to all the many kinds of truth I taught you, especially the faith and love Christ Jesus offers you.

14 Guard well that splendid ability which God has given you as a gift through the Holy Spirit Who lives within you.

15 As you know, all the Christians who came here from Asia have deserted me; even Phygellus and Hermogenes are gone.

16 May the Lord bless Onesiphorus and all his family, because he visited me and encouraged me often. His visits revived me like a breath of fresh air, and he was never ashamed of me because I am in jail.

17 In fact, when he came to Rome he searched everywhere trying to find me, and finally did.

18 May the Lord give him a special blessing at the day of Christ's return. And you know better than I can tell you how much he helped me at Ephesus.

CHAPTER 2

Oh, Timothy, my son, be strong with the strength Christ Jesus gives you.

2 For you must teach others the things which you and many witnesses have heard me speak about. Teach these great truths to trustworthy men who will, in turn, pass them on to others.

3 Take your share of suffering as a good soldier of Jesus Christ, just as I do.

4 And as Christ's soldier do not let yourself become tied up in worldly affairs, for then you cannot satisfy the One Who enlisted you in His army.

5 Follow the Lord's rules for doing His work, just as an athlete either follows the rules or is disqualified and wins no prize.

6 Work hard, like a farmer who gets paid well if he raises a large crop.

7 Think over these three illustrations, and may the Lord help you to understand them.

8 Don't ever forget the wonderful fact that Jesus

Christ was a Man, born into King David's family; and that He was God, as shown by the fact that He rose again from the dead.

9 It is because I have preached these great truths that I am in trouble here and have been put in jail like a criminal. But the Word of God is not chained, even though I am.

10 I am very willing to suffer if that will bring salvation and eternal glory in Christ Jesus to those God has chosen.

11 I am comforted by this truth, that when we suffer and die for Christ it only means that we will begin living with Him in heaven.

12 And if we think that our present service for Him is hard, just remember that someday we are going to sit with Him in heaven and rule with Him. But if we give up when we suffer, and turn against Christ, then He must turn against us.

13 Even when we are too weak to have any faith left, He remains faithful to us and will help us, for He cannot disown us who are part of Himself, and He will always carry out His promises to us.

14 Remind your people of these great facts, and command them in the name of the Lord not to argue over unimportant things. Such arguments are confusing and useless, and even harmful.

15 Work hard so God can say to you, "Well done." Be a good workman, one who does not need to be ashamed when God examines your work. Know what the Bible says and means.

16 Steer clear of foolish discussions which lead people into the sin of anger with each other.

17 Things will be said that will burn and hurt for a long time to come. Hymenaeus and Philetus, in their love of argument, are men like that.

18 They have left the path of truth, preaching the lie that the resurrection is already over; and they have weakened the faith of some who believe them.

19 But God's truth stands firm like a great rock, and nothing can shake it. And these words are written on it: "The Lord knows those who are really His," and "A person who calls himself a Christian should not be doing things that are wrong."

20 In a wealthy home there are dishes made of gold and silver as well as some made from wood and clay. The expensive dishes are used for guests, and the cheap ones are used in the kitchen or to put garbage in.

21 If you stay away from sin you will be like one of these dishes made of purest gold—the very best in the house—so that Christ Himself can use you for His highest purposes.

22 Run from anything that gives you the evil thoughts that young men often have, but stay close to anything that makes you want to do right. Have faith and love, and enjoy the companionship of those who love the Lord and have pure hearts.

23 Again I say, don't get involved in foolish arguments which only upset people and make them angry.

24 God's people must not be quarrelsome; they must be gentle, patient teachers of those who are wrong.

25 Be humble when you are trying to teach those who are mixed up concerning the truth. For if you talk meekly and courteously to them they are more likely,

with God's help, to turn away from their wrong ideas and believe what is true.

26 Then they will come to their senses and escape from Satan's trap of slavery to sin where he had caught them whenever he liked, and they can begin doing the will of God.

CHAPTER 3

You may as well know this too, Timothy, that in the last days it is going to be very difficult to be a Christian.

2 For people will love only themselves and their money; they will be proud and boastful, sneering at God, disobedient to their parents, ungrateful to them, and thoroughly bad.

3 They will be hardhearted and never give in to others; they will be constant liars and troublemakers and will think nothing of immorality. They will be rough and cruel, and sneer at those who try to be good.

4 They will betray their friends; they will be hotheaded, puffed up with pride, and prefer good times to worshiping God.

5 They will go to church, yes, but they won't really believe anything they hear. Keep far away from people like that.

6 They are the kind who craftily sneak into other people's homes and make friendships with silly, sin-burdened women and teach them their new doctrines.

7 Women of that kind are forever following new teachers, but they never understand the truth.

8 And their teachers fight truth just as Jannes and Jambres fought against Moses. They have dirty minds, warped and twisted, and have turned against the Christian faith.

9 But they won't get away with all this forever. Some day their deceit will be well-known to everyone, as was the sin of Jannes and Jambres.

10 But you know from watching me that I am not that kind of person. You know what I believe and the way I live and what I want. You know my faith in Christ and how I have suffered. You know my love for you, and my patience.

11 You know how many troubles I have had on account of the Gospel. You know all they did to me while I was visiting in Antioch, Iconium and Lystra, but the Lord delivered me.

12 Yes, and suffering will come to all who decide to live godly lives to please Christ Jesus, from those who hate Him.

13 In fact, evil men and false teachers will become worse and worse, deceiving many, they themselves deceived by Satan.

14 But you must keep on believing the things you have been taught. You know they are true for you know that you can trust those of us who have taught you.

15 You know how, when you were a small child, you were taught the holy Scriptures; and it is these that make you wise to accept God's salvation by trusting in Christ Jesus.

16 The whole Bible was given to us by inspiration from God and is useful to teach us what is true and to

make us realize what is wrong in our lives; it straightens us out and helps us do what is right.

17 It is God's way of making us well-prepared at every point, fully equipped to do good to everyone.

CHAPTER 4

And so I solemnly urge you before God and before Christ Jesus—Who will someday judge the living and the dead when He appears to set up His kingdom—

2 To preach the Word of God at all times, whenever you get the chance, in season and out, when it is convenient and when it is not. Correct and rebuke your people when they need it, encourage them to do right, and all the time be feeding them patiently with God's Word.

3 For there is going to come a time when people won't listen to the truth, but will go around looking for teachers who will tell them just what they want to hear.

4 They won't listen to what the Bible says but will gladly follow their own misguided ideas.

5 You must stay awake and watch out for all these dangers. And don't be afraid of suffering for the Lord. Bring others to Christ. Leave nothing undone that you ought to do.

6 I say this because I won't be around to help you very much longer. My time has almost run out. Very soon now I will be on my way to heaven.

7 I have fought long and hard for my Lord, and through it all I have kept true to Him. And now the time has come for me to stop fighting and rest.

8 In heaven a crown is waiting for me which the Lord, the righteous Judge, will give me on that great day of His return. And not just to me, but to all those whose lives show that they are eagerly looking forward to His coming back again.

9 Please come as soon as you can,

10 For Demas has left me. He loved the good things of this life and went to Thessalonica. Crescens has gone to Galatia, Titus to Dalmatia.

11 Only Luke is with me. Bring Mark with you when you come, for I need him.

12 (Tychicus is gone too, as I sent him to Ephesus.)

13 When you come, be sure to bring the coat I left at Troas with Brother Carpus, and also the books, but especially the parchments.

14 Alexander the coppersmith has done me much harm. The Lord will punish him,

15 But be careful of him, for he fought against everything we said.

16 The first time I was brought before the judge no one was here to help me. Everyone had run away. I hope that they will not be blamed for it.

17 But the Lord stood with me and helped me so that I could boldly preach a whole sermon for all the world to hear. And the Lord saved me from being thrown to the lions.

18 Yes, and the Lord will always deliver me from all evil and will bring me into His heavenly kingdom. To God be the glory for ever and ever. Amen.

19 Please say "hello" for me to Prisca and Aquila and those living at the home of Onesiphorus.

20 Erastus stayed at Corinth, and I left Trophimus sick at Miletum.

21 Do try to be here before winter. Eubulus sends you greetings, and so do Pudens, Linus, Claudia, and all the others.

22 May the Lord Jesus Christ be with your spirit.

Farewell,
Paul

Titus

CHAPTER 1

From: *Paul*, the slave of God and the messenger of Jesus Christ. I have been sent to bring faith to those God has chosen and to teach them to know God's truth—the kind of truth that changes lives—so that they can have eternal life, which God promised them before the world began—and He cannot lie.

3 And now in His own good time He has revealed this Good News and permits me to tell it to everyone. God our Saviour commanded that I be allowed to do this work for Him.

4 *To:* Titus, who is truly my son in the affairs of the Lord. May God the Father and Christ Jesus our Saviour give you His blessings and His peace.

5 I left you there on the island of Crete so that you could do whatever was needed to make each of its churches strong, and I asked you to appoint pastors* in every city who would follow the instructions I gave you.

6 The men you choose must be well thought of for their good lives; they must have only one wife and their children must love the Lord and not have a reputation for being wild or disobedient to their parents.

7 These pastors† must be men of blameless lives because they are God's ministers. They must not be proud, not impatient; they must not be drunkards or fighters or greedy for money.

---

†more literally, "elders" as in verse 7.

8 They must enjoy having guests in their homes and must love all that is good. They must be sensible men, and fair. They must be clean-minded and level-headed.

9 Their belief in the truth which they have been taught must be strong and steadfast, so that they will be able to teach it to others and show those who disagree with them where they are wrong,

10 For there are many who refuse to obey. This is especially true among those who say that all Christians must obey the Jewish laws. But this is foolish talk. It blinds people to the truth.

11 And it must be stopped because by it whole families are turned away from the grace of God. Those who teach like that are after your money.

12 One of their own men, a prophet born in Crete, has said about them, "These men of Crete are all liars; they are like animals—lazy and living only to fill their stomachs."

13 And this is true. So speak to them as sternly as necessary to make them strong in the faith,

14 And to stop them from listening to Jewish folk tales and the demands of men who have turned their back on the truth.

15 A person who is pure of heart sees goodness and purity in everything; but a person whose own heart is evil and untrusting finds evil in everything, for his dirty mind and rebellious heart color all he sees and hears.

16 Such persons claim they know God but from seeing the way they act, one knows they don't. They are rotten and disobedient, worthless so far as doing anything good is concerned.

CHAPTER 2

But as for you, speak up for the right living that goes along with true Christianity.

2 Teach the older men to be serious and unruffled; they must be sensible, they must know and believe the truth and do all things with love and patience.

3 Teach the older women to be quiet and respectful in everything they do. They must not go around speaking evil of others and must not be heavy drinkers, but they should be teachers of goodness.

4 These older women must train the younger women to live quietly, to love their husbands and their children,

5 And to be sensible and clean-minded, spending their time in their own homes, being kind and obedient to their husbands, so that the Christian faith can't be spoken against by those who know them.

6 In the same way urge the young men to behave carefully, taking life seriously.

7 And here you yourself must be an example to them of good deeds of every kind. Let everything you do reflect your love of the truth and the fact that you are in dead earnest about it.

8 Your conversation should be so sensible and logical that anyone who wants to argue will be ashamed of himself because there won't be anything to criticize in anything you say!

9 Urge slaves to obey their masters and do all they can to satisfy them. They must not answer back,

10 Nor steal, but must show themselves to be entirely trustworthy. In this way they will make people want to believe in our Saviour and God.

11 For the free gift of eternal salvation is now being offered to everyone;

12 And along with this gift comes the realization that God wants us to turn from godless living and from sinful pleasures and to live good, God-fearing lives day after day,

13 Looking forward to that time when His glory shall be seen—the glory of our great God and Saviour Jesus Christ,

14 Who died under God's judgment against our sins, so that He could rescue us from constant falling into sin and make us His very own people, with cleansed hearts and real enthusiasm for doing kind things for others.

15 You must teach these things and encourage your people to do them, correcting them when necessary as one who has every right to do so. Don't let anyone think that what you say is not important.

CHAPTER 3

Remind your people to obey the government and its officers, and to be always obedient, and ready for any honest work.

2 They must not speak evil of anyone, nor quarrel, but be gentle and truly courteous to all.

3 Once we were foolish and disobedient ourselves; we were misled by others and slaves to many evil pleas-

ures and wicked desires. Our lives were full of resentment and envy. We hated others and they hated us.

4 But when the time came for the goodness and loving-kindness of God our Saviour to appear,

5 Then He saved us—not because we were good enough to be saved, but because of His kindness and pity—by washing away our sins and giving us the new joy of the indwelling Holy Spirit

6 Whom He poured out upon us with wonderful fullness—and all because of what Jesus Christ our Saviour did,

7 In order that He could declare us good in God's eyes, but only because of His kindness; and now we can share in the wealth of the eternal life He gives us, and we are eagerly looking forward to receiving it.

8 These things I have told you are all true; insist on them so that Christians will be careful to do good deeds all the time, for this is not only right, but it brings results.

9 Don't get involved in arguing silly questions and queer theological ideas; keep out of arguments and quarrels about obedience to Jewish laws, for this kind of thing isn't worthwhile; it does harm.

10 If anyone is causing divisions among you, he should be given a first and second warning. After that have nothing more to do with him,

11 For such a person has a wrong sense of values. He is sinning, and knows it.

12 I am planning to send either Artemas or Tychicus to you. As soon as one of them arrives

please try to meet me at Nicopolis as quickly as you can, for I have decided to stay there for the winter.

13 Do everything you can to help Zenas the lawyer and Apollos with their trip; see that they are given everything they need.

14 For our people must learn to help all who need their assistance, that their lives will be fruitful.

15 Everybody here sends greetings. Please say "hello" to all of the Christian friends there. May God's blessings be with you all.

Sincerely,
Paul

Philemon

From: Paul, in jail for preaching the Good News about Jesus Christ, and from brother Timothy.

To: Philemon our much loved fellow worker, and to the church that meets in your home, and to Apphia our sister, and to Archippus who like myself is a soldier of the cross.

3 May God our Father and the Lord Jesus Christ give you His blessings and His peace.

4 I always thank God when I am praying for you, dear Philemon,

5 Because I keep hearing of your love and trust in the Lord Jesus and in His people.

6 And I pray that as you share your faith with others it will grip their lives too, as they see the wealth of good things in you that come from Christ Jesus.

7 I myself have gained much joy and comfort from your love, my brother, because your kindness has so often refreshed the hearts of God's people.

8, 9 Consequently I want to ask a favor of you. I could demand it of you in the name of Christ because it is the right thing for you to do, but I love you and prefer just to ask you—I, Paul, an old man now, here in jail for the sake of Jesus Christ.

10 My plea is that you show kindness to my child Onesimus, whom I won to the Lord while here in my chains.

11 Onesimus (whose name means "Useful") hasn't been of much use to you in the past, but now he is going to be of real use to both of us.

12 I am sending him back to you, and with him comes my own heart.

13 I really wanted to keep him here with me while I am in these chains for preaching the Good News, and you would have been helping me through him,

14 But I didn't want to do it without your consent. I didn't want you to be kind because you had to but because you wanted to.

15 Perhaps you could think of it this way, that he ran away from you for a little while, that now he can be yours forever,

16 No longer only a slave, but something much better—a beloved brother, especially to me. Now he will mean much more to you too, because he is not only a servant but also your brother in Christ.

17 If I am really your friend, give him the same welcome you would give me if I were there.

18 If he has harmed you in any way or stolen anything from you, charge me for it.

19 I will pay it back (I, Paul, personally guarantee this promise by writing it here with my own hand) but I won't mention how much you owe me! for you even owe me your very soul!

20 Yes dear brother, give me joy with this loving act and my weary heart will praise the Lord.

21 I've written you this letter because I am positive that you will do what I ask and even more!

22 Please keep a guest room ready for me, for I am

hoping that God will answer your prayers and let me come to you soon.

23 Epaphras my fellow prisoner, who is also here for preaching Christ Jesus, sends you his greetings.

24 So do Mark, Aristarchus, Demas and Luke, my fellow workers.

25 The blessings of our Lord Jesus Christ be upon your spirit.

Paul

Hebrews

CHAPTER 1

Long ago God spoke in many different ways to our fathers through the prophets (in visions, dreams, and even face to face)† telling them little by little about His plans.

2 But now in these days He has spoken to us through His Son to Whom He has given everything, and through Whom He made the worlds and everything there is.

3 God's Son shines out with God's glory and all that God's Son is and does marks Him as God. He holds up heaven and earth by the mighty power of His command. He is the One Who died to cleanse us and clear our record of all sin, and then sat down in highest honor beside the great God of heaven.

4 Thus He became far greater than the angels, as proved by the fact that His Name "Son of God," which was passed on to Him from His Father, is far greater than the names and titles of the angels.

5, 6 For God never said to any angel, "You are my Son, and today I have given you the honor that goes with that Name." But that is what God said about Jesus. Another time He said, "I am His Father and He is my Son." And still another time—when His firstborn Son came to earth—God said, "Let all the angels of God worship Him."

---

†implied

7 God speaks of His angels as messengers swift as the wind and as servants made of flaming fire;

8 But of His Son He says, "Your kingdom, Oh God, will last forever and ever; its commands are always just and right.

9 "You love right and hate wrong; so God, even Your God, has poured out more gladness upon You than on anyone else."

10 God also called Him "Lord" when He said, "Lord, in the beginning you made the earth, and the heavens are the work of your hands.

11 "They will disappear into nothingness, but You will remain forever. They will become worn out like old clothes,

12 "And some day You will fold them up and replace them. But You Yourself will never change, and Your years will never end."

13 And did God ever say to an angel, as He does to His Son, "Sit here beside Me in honor until I crush all Your enemies beneath Your feet?"

14 No, for the angels are only spirit-messengers sent out to help and care for those who are to receive His salvation.

CHAPTER 2

So we must listen very carefully to the truths we have heard, or we may drift away from them.

2 For since the messages from angels have always proved true and people have always been punished for disobeying them,

3 What makes us think that we can escape if we are indifferent to this great salvation announced by the Lord Jesus Himself, and passed on to us by those who heard Him speak?

4 God always has shown us that these messages are true by signs and wonders and different miracles and by giving various special abilities from the Holy Spirit to those who believe; yes, God has assigned such gifts to each of us.

5 And it is not the angels who will be in charge of the future world we are talking about:

6 No, for in the book of Psalms David says to God, "What is mere man that You are so concerned about him? and Who is this Son of Man You honor so highly?

7 "For though You made Him for a little while lower than the angels, now You have crowned Him with glory and honor.

8 "And You have put Him in complete charge of everything there is. Nothing is left out." We have not yet seen all of this take place,

9 But we do see Jesus—Who for awhile was a little lower than the angels—crowned now by God with glory and honor because He suffered death for us. Yes, because of God's great kindness, Jesus tasted death for everyone in all the world.

10 And it was right and proper that God, Who made everything for His own glory, should allow Jesus to suffer while He was bringing vast multitudes of God's people to heaven; for this suffering made Jesus a perfect leader, one fit to bring them into their salvation.

11 We who have been made holy by Jesus, now

have the same Father He has. That is why Jesus is not ashamed to call us His brothers.

12 For He says in the book of Psalms, "I will talk to my brothers about God My Father, and together we will sing His praises."

13 At another time He said, "I will put my trust in God along with my brothers." And at still another time, "See, here am I and the children God gave me."

14 Since we, God's children, are human beings—made of flesh and blood—He became flesh and blood too by being born in human form; for only as a human being could He die and in dying destroy the devil who has the power of death.

15 Only in that way could He deliver those who through fear of death have been living all their lives as slaves to constant dread.

16 We all know He did not come as an angel but as a human being, yes, a Jew.

17 And it was necessary for Jesus to be like us, His brothers, so that He could be our merciful and faithful High Priest before God, a Priest Who would be both merciful to us and faithful to God in dealing with the sins of the people.

18 For since He Himself has now been through suffering and temptation, He knows what it is like when we suffer and are tempted, and He is wonderfully able to help us.

* * * * *

CHAPTER 3

Therefore, dear brothers whom God has set apart for Himself—you who are chosen for heaven—I want you to think now about this Jesus Who is God's Messenger and the High Priest of our faith.

2 For Jesus was faithful to God Who appointed him High Priest, just as Moses also faithfully served in God's house.

3 But Jesus has far more glory than Moses, just as a man who builds a fine house gets more praise than his house does.

4 And many people can build houses, but only God made everything.

5 Well, Moses did a fine job working in God's house, but he was only a servant; and his work was mostly to illustrate and suggest those things that would happen later on.

6 But Christ is God's faithful Son in complete charge of God's house. And we Christians are God's house—He lives in us—if we keep up our courage firm to the end, and our joy and our trust in the Lord.

7, 8 And since Christ is so much superior, the Holy Spirit warns us to listen to Him, to be careful to hear His voice today and not let our hearts become set against Him as the people of Israel's were when they complained against Him in the desert, as He was testing them.

9 But God was patient with them forty years, though they tried His patience sorely, and He kept right on doing His mighty miracles for them to see.

10 "But," God says, "I was very angry with them, for their hearts were always looking somewhere else instead of up to Me, and they never found the paths I wanted them to follow."

11 Then God, full of this anger against them, bound Himself with an oath that He would never let them come to His place of rest.

12 Beware then of your own hearts, dear brothers, lest you find that they too are evil and unbelieving and are leading you away from the living God.

13 Speak to each other about these things every day while there is still time, so that none of you will become hardened against God, being blinded by the tricks of sin.

14 For if we are faithful to the end, trusting God just as we did when we first became Christians, we will share in all that belongs to Christ.

15 But *now* is the time. Never forget the warning, *"Today* if you hear God's voice speaking to you, do not harden your hearts against Him, as the people of Israel did when they rebelled against Him in the desert."

16 And who were these people I speak of, who heard God's voice speaking to them but then rebelled against Him? They were the ones who came out of Egypt with Moses their leader.

17 And who was it who made God angry for all those forty years? These same people who sinned and as a result died in the wilderness.

18 And to whom was God speaking when He swore with an oath that they could never go into the land He had promised His people? He was speaking to all those who disobeyed Him.

19 And why couldn't they go in? Because they didn't trust Him.

CHAPTER 4

Although God's promise still stands—His promise that all may enter His place of rest—we ought to tremble with fear because some of you may be on the verge of failing to get there after all.

2 For this wonderful news that God wants to save us has been given to us just as it was to those who lived in the time of Moses. But it didn't do them any good because they didn't believe it. They didn't mix it with faith.

3 For only we who believe God can enter into His place of rest. He has said, "I have sworn in my anger that those who don't believe Me will never get in," even though He has been ready and waiting for them since the world began.

4 We know He is ready and waiting because it is written that God rested on the seventh day of creation, having finished all that He had planned to make.

5 Even so they didn't get in, for God finally said, "They shall never enter my rest."

6 Yet the promise remains and some get in; not those who had the first chance, for they disobeyed God and failed to enter.

7 But He has set another time for coming in, and that time is now. He announced this through King David long years after man's first failure to enter, saying in the words already quoted, "Today when you hear Him calling, do not harden your hearts against Him."

8 This new place of rest He is talking about is not what Joshua gave to those he led into Palestine. If God had meant that, He would not have spoken long afterwards about "today" being the time to get in.

9 So there is a full, complete rest *still waiting* for the people of God.

10 Christ has already entered there. He is resting from his work, just as God Himself did.

11 Let us do our best to go into that place of rest, too, being careful not to disobey God as the children of Israel did, thus failing to get in.

12 For whatever God says to us is full of living power: It is sharper than the sharpest dagger, cutting swift and deep into our innermost thoughts and desires with all their parts, exposing us for what we really are.

13 He knows about everyone, everywhere. Everything about us is bare and wide open to the all-seeing eyes of our living God; nothing can be hidden from Him to Whom we must explain all that we have done.

14 But Jesus the Son of God is our great High Priest Who has gone to heaven itself to help us; therefore let us never stop trusting Him.

15 This High Priest of ours understands our weaknesses, since He had the same temptations we do, though He never once gave way to them and sinned.

16 So let us come boldly to the very throne of God and stay there to receive His mercy and to find grace to help us in our times of need.

CHAPTER 5

The Jewish high priest was merely a man like anyone else, but he was chosen to speak for all other men in their dealings with God; he presented their gifts to God and offered to Him the blood of animals that were sacrificed to cover the sins of the people and his own sins too. And because he was a man he could deal gently with other men, though they were foolish and ignorant, for he too was surrounded with the same temptations and understood their problems very well.

4 Another thing to remember is that no one could be a high priest just because he wanted to. He had to be called by God for this work in the same way that God chose Aaron.

5 That is why Christ did not elect Himself to the honor of being High Priest; no, He was chosen by God. God said to Him, "My Son, today I have chosen You."

6 And another time God said to Him, "You have been chosen forever as a priest with the same rank as Melchizedek."

7 Yet while Christ was here on earth He pled with God, praying with tears and agony of soul to the only One Who would save Him from (premature)† death.

†implied. Christ's longing was to live until He could die on the cross for all mankind. There is a strong case to be made that Satan's great desire was that Christ should die prematurely, before the mighty work at the cross could be performed. Christ's body, being human, was frail and weak like ours (except that His was sinless). He had said just a few days before Gethsemane, "My soul is exceeding sorrowful *unto death.*" And can a human body live long under such pressure of spirit as he underwent in the Garden, that caused sweating of great drops of blood? But God graciously heard and answered His anguished cry in Gethsemane ("Let this cup pass from me") and preserved Him from seemingly imminent and premature death: for an angel was sent to strengthen Him so that He could live to accomplish God's perfect will at the cross. . . . But some readers may prefer the explanation that Christ's plea was that He be saved *out from* death, at the Resurrection.

And God heard His prayers because of His strong desire to obey God at all times.

8 And even though Jesus was God's Son, He had to learn from experience what it was like to obey, when obeying meant suffering.

9 It was after He had proved Himself perfect in this experience that Jesus became the giver of eternal salvation to all those who obey Him.

10 For remember that God had chosen Him to be a High Priest with the same rank as Melchizedek.

11 There is much more I would like to say along these lines but you don't seem to listen, so it's hard to make you understand.

12, 13 You have been Christians a long time now, and you ought to be teaching others, but instead you have dropped back to the place where you need someone to teach you all over again the very simplest thing in God's Word. You are like babies who can drink only milk, not old enough for solid food. And when a person is still living on milk it shows he isn't very far along in the Christian life, and doesn't know much about the difference between right and wrong. He is still a baby-Christian!

14 You will never be able to eat solid spiritual food and understand the deeper things of God's Word until you become better Christians and learn right from wrong by practicing doing right.

CHAPTER 6

Let us stop going over and over again the same old ground, always teaching those first lessons about

Christ; let us go on instead to other things and become mature in our understanding, as strong Christians ought to be. Surely we don't need to speak further about the foolishness of trying to be saved by being good, or about the necessity of faith in God;

2 We don't need further instruction about baptism and church membership and the resurrection of the dead and eternal judgment.

3 The Lord willing, we will go on now to other things.

4 There is no use trying to bring you back to the Lord again if you have once understood the Good News and tasted for yourself the good things of heaven and shared in the Holy Spirit,

5 And know how good the Word of God is, and felt the mighty powers of the world to come,

6 And then have turned against God. You cannot bring yourself to repent again if you have nailed the Son of God to the cross again by rejecting Him, holding Him up to mocking and to public shame.

7 When a farmer's land has had many showers upon it and good crops come up, that land has God's blessing upon it.

8 But if it keeps on having crops of thistles and thorns, the land is considered no good and is ready for condemnation and burning off.

9 Dear friends, even though I am talking like this I really don't believe that what I am saying applies to you. I am confident you are producing the good fruit that comes along with your salvation.

10 For God is not unfair. How can He forget your

hard work for Him, or forget the way you used to show your love for Him—and still do—by helping His children?

11 And we are anxious that you keep right on loving others as long as life lasts, so that you will get your full reward.

12 Then, knowing what lies ahead for you, you won't become bored with being a Christian, nor become spiritually dull and indifferent, but you will be anxious to follow the example of those who receive all that God has promised them because of their strong faith and patience.

13 For instance, there was God's promise to Abraham: God took an oath in His own Name, since there was no one greater to swear by,

14 That He would bless Abraham again and again, and give him a son and make him the father of a great nation of people.

15 Then Abraham waited patiently until finally God gave him a son, Isaac, just as He had promised.

16 When a man takes an oath, he is calling upon someone greater than himself to force him to do what he has promised, or to punish him if he later refuses to do it; the oath ends all argument about it.

17 God also bound Himself with an oath, so that those He promised to help would know for sure and never need to wonder whether He might change His plans.

18 He has given us both His promise and His oath, two things we can completely count on, for it is impossible for God to tell a lie. Now all those who flee to

Him to save them can take new courage when they hear such assurances from God; now they can know without doubt that He will give them the salvation He has promised them.

19 This certain hope of being saved is a strong and trustworthy anchor for our souls, connecting us with God Himself behind the sacred curtains of heaven,

20 Where Christ has gone ahead to plead for us because He is forever our High Priest, with the honor and rank of Melchizedek.

CHAPTER 7

This Melchizedek was king of the city of Salem, and also a priest of the Most High God. He met Abraham when Abraham was returning home after winning a great battle against many kings, and Melchizedek blessed him.

2 Then Abraham took a tenth of all he had won in the battle and gave it to Melchizedek. Melchizedek's name means "Justice," so he is the King of Justice; and he is also the King of Peace because of the name of his city which means "Peace."

3 Melchizedek had no father or mother† and there is no record of any of his ancestors. He was never born and he never died but his life is like that of the Son of God, being a priest forever.

4 See then how great this Melchizedek is:

(a) Even Abraham, the first and most honored of

†No one can be sure whether this means that Melchizedek was Christ appearing to Abraham in human form, or simply that there is no *record* as to who Melchizedek's father or mother were, no *record* of his birth or death.

all God's chosen people, gave Melchizedek a tenth of the spoils he took from the kings he had been fighting.

5 One could understand why Abraham would do this if Melchizedek had been a Jewish priest, for later on God's people were required by law to give gifts to help their priests because the priests were their relatives.

6 But Melchizedek was not a relative, and yet Abraham paid him. (*b*) Then Melchizedek placed a blessing upon mighty Abraham,

7 And as everyone knows, a person who has the power to bless is always greater than the one he blesses.

8 (*c*) The Jewish priests who received payments from the people all died; but we read that Melchizedek lives on.

9 (*d*) One might say that Levi himself, (the father of all Jewish priests), who received tithes, paid tithes to Melchizedek through Abraham.

10 Although Levi wasn't born yet, the seed from which he came was in Abraham when Abraham paid the tithes to Melchizedek.

11 (*e*) If the Jewish priests and their laws had been able to save us, why then did God need to send Christ as a priest with the rank of Melchizedek, instead of sending someone with the rank of Aaron—the same rank all other priests had?

12-14 And when God sends a new kind of priest, His law must be changed to permit it. As we all know, Christ did not belong to the priest-tribe of Levi, but came from the tribe of Judah which had not been chosen for priesthood; Moses never gave them that work.

15 So we can plainly see that God's method

changed, for Christ the new High Priest Who came with the rank of Melchizedek

16 Did not become a priest by meeting the old requirement of belonging to the tribe of Levi, but on the basis of power flowing from a life that cannot end.

17 And the Bible points this out when it says of Christ, "You are a priest forever with the rank of Melchizedek."

18 Yes, the old system of priesthood based on family lines was canceled because it didn't work. It was weak and useless for saving people.

19 It never made anyone really right with God. But now we have a far better hope, for Christ can bring us safe to God.

20 God took an oath that Christ would always be a priest,

21 Although He never said that of other priests. But to Christ He said, "The Lord has sworn and will never change His mind: You are a priest forever, with the rank of Melchizedek."

22 Because of God's oath, Christ can guarantee forever the success of this new and better arrangement.

23 Under the old arrangement there had to be many priests because they kept dying off;

24 But Jesus lives forever and continues to be a Priest so that no one else is needed.

25 He is able to save completely all who come to God through Him. Since He will live forever, He will always be there to remind God that He has paid for their sins with His blood.

26 He is, therefore, exactly the kind of High Priest

we need; for He is holy and blameless, unstained by sin, undefiled by sinners, and to Him has been given the place of honor in heaven.

27 He never needs the daily blood of animal sacrifices, as other priests did, to cover over first their own sins and then the sins of the people; for He finished all sacrifices, once and for all, when He sacrificed Himself on the cross.

28 Under the old system, men who could not keep from doing wrong were appointed to be high priests, but later God appointed by His oath His Son Who is perfect forever.

CHAPTER 8

What I am saying is this: Christ, Whose priesthood I have just described, is our High Priest, and is in heaven at the place of greatest honor next to God Himself.

2 He ministers in the temple in heaven, the true place of worship built by the Lord and not by human hands.

3 And since every high priest is appointed to offer gifts and sacrifices, Christ must make an offering too.

4 The sacrifice He offers is far better than those offered by the earthly priests. (But even so, if He were here on earth they wouldn't even let him be a priest, because down here the priests follow the old Jewish system of sacrifices.)

5 Their work is connected with a mere earthly model of the real tabernacle in heaven; for when Moses was getting ready to build the tabernacle, God warned

him to follow exactly the pattern of the heavenly tabernacle that was shown to him on Mount Sinai.

6 But Christ, as a minister in heaven, has been rewarded with a far more important work than those who serve under the old laws, because the new agreement which He passes on to us from God contains far more wonderful promises.

7 The old agreement didn't even work. If it had, there would have been no need for another one afterwards.

8 God Himself found fault with the old one, for He said, "The day will come when I will make a new agreement with the people of Israel and the people of Judah.

9 "This new agreement will not be like the old one I gave to their fathers on the day when I took them by the hand to lead them out of the land of Egypt; they did not keep their part in that agreement, so I had to cancel it.

10 "But this is the new agreement I will make with the people of Israel, says the Lord: I will write my laws in their minds so that they will know what I want them to do without my even telling them, and these laws will be in their hearts so that they will want to obey them, and I will be their God and they shall be my people.

11 "And no one then will need to speak to his friend or neighbor or his brother, saying, 'You, too, should know the Lord,' because everyone, great and small, will know Me already.

12 "And I will be merciful to them in their wrongdoings, and I will remember their sins no more."

13 God speaks of these new promises, of this new agreement, as taking the place of the old one; for the old one is out of date now and has been put aside forever.

CHAPTER 9

Now in that first agreement between God and His people there were rules for worship and there was a sacred tent down here on earth. Inside the tent there were two rooms: the first one contained the golden candlestick and a table with special loaves of holy bread upon it. This part of the tent was called the Holy Place.

3 Then there was a curtain and behind the curtain was a room called the Holy of Holies.

4 In that room there was a golden incense-altar and the golden chest, called the ark of the convenant, completely covered on all sides with pure gold. Inside the ark were the tablets of stone with the Ten Commandments written on them, and a golden jar with some manna in it, and Aaron's wooden cane that budded.

5 Above the golden chest were statues of angels called the cherubim—the guardians of God's glory—with their wings stretched out over the ark's golden cover, called the mercy seat. But enough of such details.

6 Well, when all was ready the priests went in and out of the first room whenever they wanted to, doing their work.

7 But only the high priest went into the inner room, and then only once a year, all alone, and always with blood which he sprinkled on the mercy seat as an offering to God to cover his own mistakes and sins, and the mistakes and sins of all the people.

8 And the Holy Spirit uses all this to point out to us that under the old system the common people could not go into the Holy of Holies as long as the outer room and the old system it represents was still in use.

9 This has an important lesson for us today. For under the old system, gifts and sacrifices were offered but these failed to cleanse the hearts of the people who offered them.

10 For the old system dealt only with certain rituals, what foods to eat and drink, rules for washing themselves, and rules about this and that. The people had to keep these rules to tide them over until Christ came with God's new and better way.

11 He came as High Priest of this better system we now have. He went into that greater, perfect tabernacle in heaven, not made by men nor part of this world,

12 And once for all took blood into that inner room, the Holy of Holies, and sprinkled it on the mercy seat; but it was not the blood of goats and calves. No, He took His own blood, and with it He, by himself, made sure of our eternal salvation.

13 And if under the old system the blood of bulls and goats and the ashes of young cows could cleanse men's bodies from sin,

14 Just think how much more surely the blood of Christ will transform our lives and hearts, freeing us from the worry of having to obey the old rules and making us want to serve the living God; for by the help of the eternal Holy Spirit, Christ willingly gave Himself to God to die for our sins, He being perfect, without a single sin or fault.

15 Christ came with this new agreement so that

all who are invited may come and have forever all the wonders God has promised them. For Christ died to rescue them from the penalty of the sins they had committed while still under that old system.

16 Now, if someone dies and leaves a will—a list of things to give away to certain people when he dies—no one gets anything until it is proved that the person who wrote the will is dead.

17 The will goes into effect only after the death of the person who wrote it. While he is still alive no one can use it to get any of those things he has promised them.

18 That is why blood was sprinkled (as proof of Christ's death)† before even those first promises went into effect.

19 For after Moses had given the people all of God's laws, he took the blood of calves and goats, along with water, and sprinkled the blood over the book of God's laws and over all the people, using branches of hyssop bushes and scarlet wool to sprinkle with.

20 Then he said, "This is the blood that marks the beginning of the agreement between you and God, the agreement God commanded me to make with you."

21 And in the same way he sprinkled blood on the holy tent and on whatever was used for worship.

22 In fact we can say that under the old agreement almost everything was cleansed by sprinkling it with blood, and without the shedding of blood there is no forgiveness of sins.

23 That is why the sacred tent down here on earth,

†implied.

and everything in it—all copied from things in heaven—had to be made pure by Moses in this way, by sprinkling them with the blood of animals. But the real things in heaven of which these down here are copies, were made pure with far more precious offerings.

24 For Christ has entered into heaven itself, to appear now before God as our friend. It was not in the earthly, sacred tent that He did this, for that was merely a copy of the real one in heaven.

25 Nor has He offered Himself again and again, as the high priest down here on earth offered animal blood in the Holy of Holies each year.

26 If that had been necessary, then He would have had to die again and again, ever since the world began. But no! He came once for all, at the close of the age, to put away the power of sin forever by dying for us.

27 And just as it is destined that men die only oncc, and after that comes judgment,

28 So also Christ died only once as an offering for the sins of many people; and He will come again, but not to deal again with our sins. This time He will come bringing salvation to all those who are eagerly and patiently waiting for Him.

CHAPTER 10

The old system of Jewish laws gave only a dim foretaste of the good things Christ would do for us. The sacrifices under the old system were repeated again and again, year after year, but even so they could never save those who lived under their rules.

2 Otherwise one offering would have been enough; the worshipers would have been cleansed once for all time, and their feeling of guilt would be gone.

3 Rather, those yearly sacrifices reminded them of their guilt and wickedness instead of relieving their minds.

4 For it is not possible for the blood of bulls and goats to really take away sins.†

5 That is why Christ said, as He came into the world, "O God, the blood of bulls and goats cannot satisfy You, so You have made ready this body of mine for me to lay as a sacrifice upon Your altar.

6 "You were not satisfied with the animal sacrifices, slain and burnt before You as offerings for sin.

7 "Then I said, 'See, I have come to lay down my life, just as the Scriptures have said that I would.' "

8 After Christ said this, about not being satisfied with the various sacrifices and offerings required under the old system,

9 He then added, "See, I have come to give my life." He cancels the first system in favor of a far better one.

10 Under this new plan we have been forgiven and made clean by Christ dying for us once and for all.

11 Under the old agreement the priests stood there day after day offering sacrifices that could never take away our sins.

12 But Christ gave Himself as one sacrifice to God

---

†The blood of bulls and goats merely covered over the sins, taking them out of sight for hundreds of years until Jesus Christ came to die on the cross. There He gave His own blood which forever took those sins away.

for our sins, and then sat down in the place of highest honor at God's right hand,

13 Waiting for His enemies to be laid under His feet.

14 For by that one offering He made forever perfect in the sight of God all those whom He is making holy.

15 And the Holy Spirit testifies that this is so, for He has said,

16 "This is the agreement I will make with the people of Israel, though they broke their first agreement. I will write my laws into their minds so that they will always know my will and I will put my laws in their hearts so that they will want to obey them."

17 And then He adds, "I will never again remember their sins and lawless deeds."

18 Now, when sins have once been forever forgiven and forgotten, there is no need to offer more sacrifices to get rid of them.

19 And so, dear brothers, now we may walk right into the very Holy of Holies where God is, because of the blood of Jesus.

20 This is the fresh, new, life-giving way which Christ has opened up for us by tearing the curtain—His human nature—to let us into the holy presence of God.

21 And since this great High Priest of our rules over God's household,

22 Let us go right in, to God Himself, with true hearts fully trusting Him to receive us, because we have been sprinkled with Christ's blood to make us clean, and

because we have been washed with the pure water of baptism by the Holy Spirit.

23 Now we can look forward without doubting to the salvation God has promised us, and we can tell others it is ours, for there is no question that He will do what He says.

24 In response to all He has done for us, let us outdo each other in being helpful and being kind to each other and doing good.

25 Let us not neglect our church duties and meetings, as some people do, but encourage and warn each other, especially now that the Day of His coming back again is drawing near.

26 If anyone sins deliberately by rejecting the Saviour after knowing the truth of forgiveness, this sin is not covered by Christ's death; there is no way to get rid of it.

27 There will be nothing left to look forward to but terrible punishment and God's awful anger which will consume all His enemies.

28 A man who refused to obey the laws given by Moses was killed without mercy if there were two or three witnesses to his sin.

29 Think how much more terrible the punishment will be for those who have trampled underfoot the Son of God and treated His cleansing blood as though it were common and unhallowed, thus insulting and outraging the Holy Spirit Who brings God's mercy to His people.

30 For we know Him Who said, "Justice belongs to me; I will repay them;" Who also said "The Lord Himself will handle these cases."

31 It is a fearful thing to fall into the hands of the living God.

32 Don't ever forget those wonderful days of old when you first learned about Christ. Remember how you kept right on with the Lord even though it meant terrible suffering.

33 Sometimes you were laughed at and beaten, and sometimes you watched and sympathized with others suffering the same things.

34 You suffered with those thrown into jail, and you were actually joyful when all you owned was taken from you, knowing that better things were awaiting you in heaven, things that would be yours forever.

35 Do not let this happy trust in the Lord die away no matter what happens. Remember your reward!

36 You need to keep on patiently doing God's will if you want Him to do for you all that He has promised.

37 His coming will not be much longer delayed.

38 And those whose faith has made them good in God's sight must live by faith, trusting Him in everything. Otherwise, if they shrink back, God will have no pleasure in them.

39 But we have never turned our backs on God and sealed our fate. No, our faith in Him assures our souls' salvation.

CHAPTER 11

What is faith? It is the confident assurance that something we want is going to happen. It is the certainty that what we hope for is waiting for us, even though we cannot see it up ahead.

2 Men of God in days of old were famous for their faith.

3 By faith—because we believe God—we know that the world and the stars, in fact all things, were made at God's command; and that they were made from nothing!

4 It was by faith that Abel obeyed God and brought an offering that pleased God more than Cain's offering did. God accepted Abel and proved it by accepting his gift; and though Abel is long dead, we can still learn lessons from him about trusting God.

5 Enoch trusted God too and that is why He took him away to heaven without dying. Suddenly he was gone because God took him. For God had said before this happened how pleased He was with Enoch.

6 You can never please God without faith, without depending on Him. Anyone who wants to come to God must believe that there is a God and that He will reveal Himself to those who sincerely look for Him.

7 Noah was another who trusted God. When he heard God's warning about the future, Noah believed Him even though there was then no sign of a flood, and wasting no time, he built the ark and saved his family. By believing God, Noah showed up the sin of the rest of the world—which refused to obey—and because of his faith he became one of those God accepts.

8 Abraham trusted God, and when God told him to leave home and go far away to another land which He promised to give him, Abraham obeyed. Away he went, not even knowing where he was going.

9 And even when he reached God's promised land,

he lived in tents like a mere visitor, as did Isaac and Jacob, to whom God gave the same promise.

10 Abraham did this because he was confidently waiting for God to bring him to that strong heavenly city whose designer and builder is God.

11 Sarah too had faith, and because of this she was able to become a mother in spite of her old age, for she realized that God, Who gave her His promise, would certainly do what He said.

12 And so a whole nation came from Abraham, who was too old to have even one child; a nation with so many millions of people that, like the stars of the sky and the sand on the ocean shores, there is no way to count them.

13 These people I have mentioned died while trusting the Lord without ever getting all God had promised them, but they saw all He had promised awaiting them on ahead and were glad, for they agreed that this earth was not their real home but that they were just strangers visiting down here.

14 And quite obviously when they talked like that they were looking forward to their real home in heaven.

15 If they had wanted to, they could have gone back to the good things of this world.

16 But they didn't want to. They were living for heaven. And now God is not ashamed to be called their God, for He has made a heavenly city for them.

17 When God was testing him, Abraham still trusted in God and His promises, and so he offered up his son Isaac, and was ready to slay him on the altar of sacrifice,

18 Yes, to slay even Isaac, through whom God had promised to give Abraham a whole nation of descendants!

19 He believed that if Isaac died God would bring him back to life again; and that is just about what happened, for as far as Abraham was concerned, Isaac was doomed to death, but he came back again alive!

20 It was by faith that Isaac knew God would give future blessings to his two sons, Jacob and Esau.

21 By faith Jacob, when he was old and dying, blessed each of Joseph's two sons as he stood and prayed, leaning on the top of his cane.

22 And it was by faith that Joseph, as he neared the end of his life, confidently spoke of God bringing the people of Israel out of Egypt; and he was so sure of it that he made them promise to carry his bones with them when they left!

23 Moses' parents had faith too. When they saw that God had given them an unusual child, they trusted that God would save him from the death the king commanded, and they hid him for three months, and were not afraid.

24, 25 It was by faith that Moses, when he grew up, refused to be treated as the grandson of the king, but chose to share ill treatment with God's people instead of enjoying the fleeting pleasures of sin.

26 He thought that it was better to suffer for Christ than to own all the money in Egypt, for he was looking forward to the great reward that God would give him.

27 And it was because he trusted God that he left the land of Egypt and wasn't afraid of the king's anger.

Moses kept right on going; it seemed as though he could see God right there with him.

28 And it was because he believed God would take care of His people that he commanded them to kill a lamb as God had told them to, and sprinkle the blood on the doorposts of their homes so that God's terrible angel of death could not touch the oldest child in those homes, as he did among the Egyptians.

29 The people of Israel trusted God and went right through the Red Sea as though they were on dry ground. But when the Egyptians tried it, they were all drowned.

30 It was faith that brought the walls of Jericho tumbling down after the people of Israel had walked around them seven days, as God had commanded them.

31 By faith—because she believed in God and His power—Rahab the harlot did not die with all the others in her city when they refused to obey God, for she gave a friendly welcome to the spies.

32 Well, how much more do I need to say? It would take too long to tell the stories of the faith of Gideon and Barak and Samson and Jephthah and David and Samuel and the prophets.

33 These people all trusted God and as a result won battles, overthrew kingdoms, ruled their people well, and received what God had promised them; they were kept from harm in a den of lions,

34 And in a fiery furnace. Some, through their faith, escaped death by the sword. Some were made strong again after they had been weak or sick. Others were given great power in battle; they made whole armies turn and run away.

35 And some women, through faith, received their loved ones back again from death.

But others trusted God and were beaten to death, preferring to die rather than turn from God and be free—trusting that they would rise again to a better life afterwards.

36 Others were laughed at and their backs cut open with whips, and some were chained in dungeons.

37, 38 Some died by stoning and some by being sawed in two; others were promised freedom if they would deny Christ, then were killed with the sword. Some went about in skins of sheep and goats, wandering over deserts and mountains, hiding in dens and caves. They were hungry and sick and ill-treated—too good for this world.

39 Though they trusted God and won His approval, they didn't receive all God had promised them;

40 For God had arranged even better rewards for us and He wanted them to wait and share them with us.

CHAPTER 12

Since we have such a huge crowd of men of faith watching us from the grandstands, let us strip off anything that slows us down or holds us back, and especially those sins that wrap themselves so tightly around our feet and trip us up; and let us run with patience the particular race that God has set before us.

2 Keep your eyes on Jesus, our leader and instructor. He was willing to die a shameful death on the cross because of the joy He knew would be His

afterwards; and now He sits in the place of honor by the throne of God.

3 If you want to keep from becoming fainthearted and weary, think about His patience as sinful men did such terrible things to Him.

4 After all, you have never yet struggled against sin and temptation until you sweat great drops of blood.

5 And have you quite forgotten the encouraging words God spoke to you, His child? He said, "My son, don't be angry when the Lord punishes you. Don't be discouraged when He has to show you where you are wrong.

6 "For when He punishes you, it proves that He loves you. When He whips you it proves you are really His child."

7 Let God train you, for He is doing what any loving father does for his children. For whoever heard of a son who was never corrected?

8 If God doesn't punish you when you need it, as other fathers punish their sons, then it means that you aren't really God's son at all—that you don't really belong in His family.

9 Since we respect our fathers here on earth, though they punish us, should we not all the more cheerfully submit to God's training so that we can begin to really live?

10 Our earthly fathers trained us for a few brief years, doing the best for us that they knew how, but God's correction is always right and for our best good, that we may share His holiness.

11 Being punished isn't enjoyable while it is hap-

pening—it hurts! But afterwards we can see the result, a quiet growth in grace and character.

12 So take a new grip with your tired hands, stand firm on your shaky legs,

13 And mark out a straight, smooth path for your feet so that those who follow you, though weak and lame, will not fall and hurt themselves, but become strong.

* * * * *

14 Try to stay out of all quarrels and seek to live a clean and holy life, for one who is not holy will not see the Lord.

15 Look after each other so that not one of you will fail to find God's best blessings. Watch out that no bitterness takes root among you, for as it springs up it causes deep trouble, hurting many in their spiritual lives.

16 Watch out that no one becomes involved in sexual sin or becomes careless about God as Esau did: for a single meal he sold his rights as the oldest son.

17 And remember that afterwards when he wanted them back again it was too late, though he wept bitter tears of repentance.

* * * * *

18 You have not had to stand face to face with terror, flaming fire, gloom, and darkness and a terrible storm, as the Israelites did at Mount Sinai when God gave them His laws.

19 For there was an awesome trumpet blast, and a voice with a message so terrible that the people begged God to stop speaking.

20 They staggered back under God's command that if even an animal touched the mountain it must die.

21 Moses himself was so frightened at the sight that he shook with terrible fear.

22 But you have come right up into Mount Zion, to the city of the living God, the heavenly Jerusalem; and to the gathering of countless happy angels;

23 And to the church, composed of all those registered in heaven; and to God who is Judge of all; and to the spirits of the redeemed in heaven, already made perfect;

24 And to Jesus Himself, Who has brought us His wonderful new agreement; and to the sprinkled blood which graciously forgives instead of crying out for vengeance as the blood of Abel did.

25 So see to it that you obey Him Who is speaking to you. For if the people of Israel did not escape when they refused to listen to Moses, the earthly messenger, how terrible our danger if we refuse to listen to God Who speaks to us from heaven.

26 When He spoke from Mount Sinai His voice shook the earth, but, "Next time," He says, "I will not only shake the earth, but the heavens too."

27 By this He means that He will sift out everything without solid foundations, so that only unshakable things will be left.

28 Since we have a kingdom nothing can destroy, let us please God by serving Him with thankful hearts, and with holy fear and awe.

29 For our God is a consuming fire.

CHAPTER 13

Continue to love each other with true brotherly love.

2 Don't forget to be kind to strangers, for some who have done this have entertained angels without realizing it!

3 Don't forget about those in jail. Suffer with them as though you were there yourself. Share the sorrow of those being mistreated, for you know what they are going through.

* * * * *

4 Honor your marriage and its vows; and be pure; for God will surely punish all those who are immoral or commit adultery.

* * * * *

5 Stay away from the love of money; be satisfied with what you have. For God has said, "I will never fail you nor forsake you."

6 That is why we can say without any doubt or fear, "The Lord is my Helper and I am not afraid of anything that man can do to me."

7 Remember your leaders who have taught you the Word of God. Think of all the good that has come from their lives, and try to trust the Lord as they do.

* * * * *

8 Jesus Christ is the same yesterday, today and forever.

9 So do not be attracted by strange, new ideas, for your spiritual strength comes as a gift from God, not from ceremonial rules about eating certain foods—a

method which, by the way, hasn't helped those who have tried it!

* * * * *

10 We have an altar—the cross where Christ was sacrificed—where those who continue to seek salvation by obeying Jewish laws can never be helped.

11 Under the system of Jewish laws the high priest brought the blood of the slain animals into the sanctuary as a sacrifice for sin, and then the bodies of the animals were burned outside the city.

12 That is why Jesus suffered and died outside the city, where His blood washed our sins away.

13 So let us go out to Him beyond the city walls (that is, outside the interests of this world, being willing to be despised)† to suffer with him there, bearing His shame.

14 For this world is not our home; we are looking forward to our everlasting home in heaven.

* * * * *

15 With Jesus' help we will continually offer our sacrifice of praise to God by telling others of the glory of His name.

16 Don't forget to do good and to share what you have with those in need, for such sacrifices are very pleasing to Him.

* * * * *

17 Obey your leaders and be willing to do what they say. For their work is to watch over your souls, and God will judge them on how well they do this. Give them reason to report joyfully about you to the Lord and

†implied.

not with sorrow, for then you will suffer for it too.

18 Pray for us, for our conscience is clear and we want to keep it that way.

19 I especially need your prayers right now so that I can come back to you the sooner.

* * * * *

20, 21 And now may the God of peace Who brought again from the dead our Lord Jesus, the great Shepherd of the sheep, equip you with all you need for doing His will, through the blood of the everlasting agreement between God and you. And may He produce in you through the power of Christ all that is pleasing to Him: to Whom be glory forever and ever. Amen.

* * * * *

22 Brethren, please listen patiently to what I have said in this letter, for it is a short one.

23 I want you to know that brother Timothy is now out of jail; if he comes here soon, I will come with him to see you.

24 Give my greetings to all your leaders and to the others there. The Christians from Italy who are here with me send you their love. God's grace be with you all. Amen.

James

CHAPTER 1

F*rom:* James: a servant of God and of the Lord Jesus Christ.

To: Jewish Christians scattered everywhere. Greetings!

2 Dear brothers, is your life full of difficulties and temptations? Then be happy,

3 For when the way is rough, your patience has a chance to grow.

4 So let it grow, and don't try to squirm out of your problems. For when your patience is finally in full bloom, then you will be ready for anything, strong in character, full and complete.

5 If you want to know what God wants you to do, ask Him, and He will gladly tell you, for He is always ready to give a bountiful supply of wisdom to all who ask Him; He will not resent it.

6 But when you ask Him, be sure that you really expect Him to tell you, for a doubtful mind will be as unsettled as a wave of the sea that is driven and tossed by the wind,

7, 8 And every decision you then make will be uncertain, as you turn first this way, and then that. So if you don't ask with faith, don't expect the Lord to give you any solid answers.

9 A Christian who doesn't amount to much in this world should be glad, for he is great in the Lord's sight.

10, 11 But a rich man should be glad that his riches mean nothing to the Lord, for he will soon be gone, like a flower that has lost its beauty and fades away, withered—killed by the scorching summer sun. So it is with rich men. They will soon die and leave behind all their busy activities.

12 Happy is the man who doesn't give in and do wrong when he is tempted, for afterwards he will get as his reward the crown of life that God has promised those who love Him.

13 And remember, when someone wants to do wrong it is never God who is tempting him, for God never wants to do wrong and never tempts anyone else to do it.

14 But temptation is the pull of man's own evil thoughts and wishes.

15 Then the evil thoughts lead to evil actions and afterwards to the death penalty from God.

16 So don't be misled dear brothers.

17 But whatever is good and perfect comes to us from God, the Creator of all light, and He shines forever without change or shadow.

18 And it was a happy day for Him† when He gave us our new lives, through the truth of His Word, and we became, as it were, the first children in His new family.

19 Dear brothers, don't ever forget that it is best to listen much, speak little, and not become angry;

†literally: "Of His own free will He gave us, etc."

20 For anger doesn't make us good, as God demands that we must be.

21 So get rid of all that is wrong in your life, both inside and outside, and humbly be glad for the wonderful message we have received, for it is able to save our souls as it grows in our hearts.

22 And remember, it is a message to obey, not just to listen to. So don't fool yourselves:

23 For if a person just listens and doesn't obey, he is like a man looking at his face in a mirror;

24 As soon as he walks away, he can't see himself anymore or remember what he looks like.

25 But if he keeps looking steadily into God's law for free men he will not only remember it, but do what it says, and God will greatly bless that man in everything he does.

26 If anyone says he is a Christian but doesn't control his sharp tongue, he is just fooling himself and his religion isn't worth much.

27 The Christian who is pure and without fault, from God the Father's point of view, is the one who takes care of orphans and widows, and whose soul remains true to the Lord—not soiled and dirtied by its contacts with the world.

CHAPTER 2

Dear brothers, how can you claim that you belong to the Lord Jesus Christ, the Lord of glory, if you show favoritism to rich people and look down on poor people?

2 If a man comes into your church dressed in expensive clothes and with valuable gold rings on his fingers, and at the same moment another man comes in who is poor and dressed in threadbare clothes,

3 And you make a lot of fuss over the rich man and give him the best seat in the house and say to the poor man, "You can stand over there if you like, or else sit on the floor"—well,

4 This kind of action casts a question mark across your faith—are you really a Christian at all?—and shows that you are guided by evil motives.

5 Listen to me, dear brothers: God has chosen poor people to be rich in faith, and the kingdom of heaven is theirs, for that is the gift God has promised to those who love Him.

6 And yet, of the two strangers, you have despised the poor man. Don't you realize that it is usually the rich men who pick on you and drag you into court?

7 And all too often they are the ones who laugh at Jesus Christ, whose noble name you bear.

8 Yes indeed, it is good when you truly obey our Lord's command, "You must love and help your neighbors just as much as you love and take care of yourself."

9 But you are breaking this law of our Lord's when you favor the rich and fawn over them; it is sin.

10 And the person who keeps every law of God, but makes one little slip, is just as guilty as the person who has broken every law there is.

11 For the God Who said you must not marry a woman who already has a husband, also said you must not murder, so even though you have not broken the

marriage laws by committing adultery, but have murdered someone, you have entirely broken God's laws and stand utterly guilty before Him.

12 You will be judged on whether or not you are doing what Christ wants you to. So watch what you do and what you think;

13 For there will be no mercy to those who have shown no mercy. But if you have been merciful, then God's mercy towards you will win out over His judgment against you.

14 Dear brothers, what's the use of saying that you have faith and are Christians if you aren't proving it by helping others? Will *that* kind of faith save anyone?

15 If you have a friend who is in need of food and clothing

16 And you say to him, "Well, goodbye and God bless you, stay warm and eat hearty," and then don't give him clothes or food, what good does that do?

17 So you see, it isn't enough just to have faith. You must also do good to prove that you have faith. Faith without good deeds is dead and useless.

18 But someone may say, "You think the way to God is by faith alone, plus nothing; well, I say that good deeds are important too, for without good deeds you cannot show me whether you have faith or not; but anyone can see that I believe by the way I act."

19 You think "believing" is enough, do you? Believing in one God? Well, remember that the devils believe this too, and believe it so strongly that they tremble in terror!

20 Dear foolish man! When will you ever learn

that "believing" is useless without *doing* what God wants you to? Faith that does not result in good deeds is not real faith.

21 Don't you remember that even father Abraham was declared good because of what he *did,* when he was willing to obey God, even if it meant offering his son Isaac to die on the altar?

22 You see, he was trusting God so much that he was willing to do whatever God told him to; his faith was made complete by what he did, by his actions, his good deeds.

23 And so it happened just as the Scriptures say, that Abraham trusted God, and the Lord declared him good in God's sight, and he was even called "The Friend of God."

24 So you see, a man is saved by what he does, as well as by what he believes.

25 Rahab, the wicked woman, is another example of this. She was saved because of what she did when she hid those messengers and sent them safely away by a different road.

26 Just as the body is dead when there is no spirit in it, so faith is dead if it is not the kind that results in good deeds.

CHAPTER 3

Dear brothers, don't be too eager to tell others their faults,† for we all make many mistakes; and when we teachers, who should know better, do wrong, our punishment will be greater than it would be for others;

†literally: "Not many (of you) should become masters (teachers)."

2 If anyone can control his tongue, it proves that he has perfect control over himself in every other way.

3 We can make a large horse turn around and go wherever we want by means of a small bit in his mouth.

4 And a tiny rudder makes a huge ship turn wherever the pilot wants it to go, even though the wind is strong.

5 So also the tongue is a small thing, but what terrible results it can cause. A great forest can be set on fire by one tiny spark.

6 And the tongue is a flame of fire. It is full of wickedness and poisons every part of the body. And the tongue is set on fire by hell itself, and can turn our whole lives into a blazing flame of destruction and disaster.

7 Men have trained, or can train, every kind of animal or bird that lives and every kind of snake and fish,

8 But no human being can tame the tongue. It is always ready to pour out its deadly poison.

9 Sometimes it praises our heavenly Father, and sometimes it breaks out into curses against men who are made like God.

10 And so blessing and cursing come pouring out of the same mouth. Dear brothers, surely this is not right!

11 Does a spring of water bubble out first with fresh water and then with bitter water?

12 Can you pick olives from a fig tree, or figs from a grape vine? No, and you can't draw fresh water from a salty pool.

13 If you are wise, live a life of steady goodness,

so that only good deeds will pour forth. And if you don't brag about them, then you will be truly wise!

14 And by all means don't brag about being wise and good if you are bitter and jealous and selfish; that is the worst sort of lie.

15 For jealousy and selfishness are not God's kind of wisdom. Such things are earthly, unspiritual, inspired by the devil, and come from hell itself.

16 For wherever there is jealousy or selfish ambition, there will be disorder and every other kind of evil.

17 But the wisdom that comes from heaven is first of all pure and full of quiet gentleness. Then it is peace-loving and courteous. It allows discussion and is willing to yield to others; it is full of mercy and good deeds. It is wholehearted and straightforward and sincere.

18 And those who are peacemakers will plant seeds of peace and reap a harvest of goodness.

CHAPTER 4

What is causing the quarrels and fights among you? Isn't it because there is a whole army of evil desires within you?

2 You want what you don't have so you kill to get it. You long for what others have, and can't afford it, so you start a fight to take it away from them. And yet the reason you don't have what you want is because you don't ask God for it.

3 And when you do ask you don't get it because your whole aim is wrong—you want only what will give *you* pleasure.

4 You are like an unfaithful wife who loves her husband's enemies. Don't you realize that making friends with God's enemies—the evil pleasures of this world—makes God your enemy? I say it again, that if your aim is to enjoy the evil pleasure of the unsaved world, you cannot also be a friend of God.

5 Or what do you think the Scriptures mean when they say that the Holy Spirit, Whom God has placed within us, watches over us with tender jealousy?

6 But He gives us strength to stand against all such evil longings. As the Scriptures say, God gives strength to the humble but sets Himself against the proud and haughty.

7 So give yourselves humbly to God. Resist the devil and he will flee from you.

8 And when you draw close to God, God will draw close to you. Wash your hands, oh sinners, and fill your hearts with God alone to make them pure and true to Him.

9 Let there be tears for the wrong things you have done. Let there be sorrow and sincere grief. Let there be sadness instead of laughter and gloom instead of joy.

10 Then when you feel your worthlessness before the Lord, He will lift you up, encourage and help you.

11 Don't criticize and speak evil about each other, dear brothers. If you do, you will be fighting against God's law of loving one another, declaring it is wrong. But your job is to obey the law, not to decide whether it is right or wrong.

12 And He alone, Who made the law, can rightly judge among us. He alone decides to save us or destroy.

So what right do you have to judge or criticize others?

13 Look here, you people who say "Today or tomorrow we are going to such and such a town, stay there a year, and open up a profitable business."

14 How do you know what is going to happen tomorrow? For the length of your lives is as uncertain as the morning fog; now you see it, soon it is gone.

15 What you ought to say is "If the Lord wants us to, we shall live and do this or that."

16 Otherwise you will be bragging about your own plans, and such self-confidence never pleases God.

17 Remember too that knowing what is right to do and then not doing it is sin.

CHAPTER 5

Look here, you rich men, now is the time to cry and groan with violent grief in view of all the terrible troubles ahead of you.

2 For your wealth is rotting away, and your fine clothes are becoming moth-eaten rags.

3 The value of your gold and silver is dropping fast, yet it will stand as evidence against you, and eat your flesh like fire. That is what you have stored up for yourselves in that coming day of judgment.

4 For listen! Hear the cries of the field workers whom you have cheated of their pay. Their cries have reached the ears of the Lord of Hosts.

5 You have spent your years here on earth having fun, satisfying your every whim, and now your fat hearts are ready for the slaughter.

6 You have condemned and killed good men who had no power to defend themselves against you.

7 But on the other hand, you, dear brothers, be patient until the Lord returns. Be like a patient farmer who expects to wait until the autumn for his precious harvest to ripen.

8 Yes, be patient. And take courage, for the coming of the Lord is near.

9 Don't grumble about each other, brothers. Are you yourselves above criticism? For see! the great Judge is coming. He is almost here; (let Him do whatever criticizing must be done).

10 For examples of patience in suffering, look at the Lord's prophets.

11 We know how happy they are now because they stayed true to Him then, even though they suffered greatly for it. Job is an example of a man who continued to trust the Lord in sorrow, and from his experiences we can see how the Lord's plan finally ended in good, and that the Lord is full of tenderness and mercy.

12 But most of all, dear brothers, do not swear either by heaven or earth or anything else; just say a simple "yes," or "no," so that you will not sin and receive God's curse.

13 Is anyone among you suffering? He should keep on praying about it; and those who have reason to be thankful should continually be singing praises to the Lord.

14 Is anyone sick? He should call for the elders of the church and they should pray over him and pour a little oil upon him, calling on the Lord to heal him.

15 And their prayer, if offered in faith, will heal him, for the Lord will make him well; and if his sickness was caused by some sin, the Lord will forgive him.

16 Admit your faults to one another and pray for each other so that you may be healed. The earnest prayer of a righteous man has great power and wonderful results.

17 Elijah was as perfectly human as we are, and yet when he prayed earnestly that no rain would fall, none fell for the next three and one half years!

18 Then he prayed again, this time that it *would* rain, and down it poured and the grass turned green and the gardens began to grow again.

19 Dear brothers, if anyone has slipped way from God and no longer trusts the Lord, and someone helps him understand the Truth again,

20 That person who brings him back to God will save a wandering soul from death and bring about the forgiveness of his many sins.

I Peter

CHAPTER 1

From: Peter, Jesus Christ's missionary.

To: The Jewish Christians driven out of Jerusalem and scattered throughout Pontus, Galatia, Cappadocia, Asia and Bithynia.

2 Dear friends, God the Father chose you long ago and knew you would become His children. And the Holy Spirit has been at work in your hearts, cleansing them with the blood of Jesus Christ and making you anxious to please Him. May God bless you richly and grant you increasing freedom from all anxiety and fear.

3 All honor to God, the God and Father of our Lord Jesus Christ, for His boundless mercy to us, so that we have been born again, and are now members of God's own family. Now we live in the hope of eternal life because Christ rose again from the dead.

4 And He has reserved for His children the priceless gift of salvation; it is kept in heaven for you, pure and undefiled, beyond the reach of change and decay.

5 And God, in His mighty power, will make sure that you get there safely to receive it, because you are trusting Him. It will be yours in that coming last day for all to see.

6 So be truly glad! There is wonderful joy ahead, even though the going is rough for a while down here.

7 This only tests your faith, that you may see whether it is strong and pure or not. It is being tested as fire tests gold and purifies it—and your faith is far more precious to God than mere gold; so if your faith remains strong after being in the test tube of fiery trials, it will bring you much praise and glory and honor on the day of His return.

8 You love Him even though you have never seen Him; though not seeing Him, you trust Him; and even now you are happy with the inexpressible joy that comes from heaven itself.

9 And your further reward for trusting Him will be the salvation of your souls.

10 This salvation was something the prophets did not understand. They wrote about it, but they had many questions as to what it all could mean.

11 They wondered what the Spirit of Christ within them was talking about, for He told them to write down the events which, since then, have happened to Christ: His suffering, and His great glory afterwards. And they wondered when and to Whom all this would happen.

12 They were finally told that these things would not occur during their lifetime, but long years later, during yours. And now at last this Good News has been plainly announced to all of us. It was preached to us in the power of the same heaven-sent Holy Spirit Who spoke to them; and it is all so strange and wonderful that even the angels in heaven would give a great deal to know more about it.

13 So now you can look forward soberly and in-

telligently to more of God's kindness to you when Jesus Christ returns.

14 Obey God because you are His children; don't slip back into your old ways—doing evil because you knew no better.

15 But in all you do be holy, now, as the Lord is, Who invited you to be His child.

16 For the Lord has said, "You must be holy, for I am holy."

17 And remember that your heavenly Father to Whom you pray has no favorites when He judges. He will judge you with perfect justice for everything you do; so act in reverent fear of Him from now on until you get to heaven.

18 God paid a ransom to save you from the impossible road to heaven which your fathers tried to take, and the ransom He paid was not mere gold or silver, as you very well know,

19 But He paid for you with the precious lifeblood of Christ, the sinless, spotless Lamb of God.

20 God chose Him for this purpose long before the world began, but only recently was He brought into public view, in these last days, as a blessing to you.

21 Because of this your trust can be in God Who raised Christ from the dead and gave Him great glory. Now your faith and hope can rest in Him alone.

22 Now you can have real love for everyone because your souls have been cleansed from selfishness and hatred when you trusted Christ to save you; so see to it that you really do love each other warmly, with all your hearts.

23 For you have a new life. It was not passed on to you from your parents, for the life they gave you will fade away. This new one will last forever, for it comes from Christ, God's ever-living Message to men.

24 Yes, our natural lives will fade as grass does, when it becomes all brown and dry; and all our greatness is like a flower that droops and falls;

25 But the Word of the Lord will last forever. And His message is the Good News that was preached to you.

CHAPTER 2

So get rid of your feelings of hatred. Don't just pretend to be good! Be done with dishonesty and jealousy and talking about others behind their backs.

2, 3 If you have tasted the Lord's goodness and kindness, cry for more, as a baby cries for milk. Eat God's Word—read it, think about it—and grow strong in the Lord.

4 Come to Christ Who is the living Foundation of Rock upon which God builds; though men have spurned Him, He is very precious to God Who has chosen Him above all others.

5 And now you have become living building blocks of stone for God's use in building His house; and you are also His holy priests; so come to Him there, with Jesus Christ, and offer to God those things that please Him well.

6 As the Scriptures express it, "See, I am sending Christ to be the carefully chosen, precious Cornerstone of my church, and I will never disappoint those who trust in Him."

7 Yes, He is very precious to you who believe; and to those who reject Him, well, "the same Stone that was rejected by the builders has become the Cornerstone, the most honored and important part of the building."

8 And the Scriptures also say, "He is the Stone that some will stumble over, and the Rock that will make them fall." They will stumble because they will not listen to God's Word, nor obey it, and so this punishment must follow: that they will fall.

9 But you are not like that, for you have been chosen by God Himself; you are priests of the King, you are holy and pure, you are God's very own—and all this that you may show to others how God called you out of darkness into His wonderful light.

10 Once you were less than nothing, now you are God's own. Once you knew very little of God's kindness, now your very lives have been changed by it.

11 Dear brothers, you are only visitors here. Since your real home is in heaven I beg you to keep away from the evil pleasures of this world; they are not for you, for they fight against your very souls.

12 Be careful how you behave among your unsaved neighbors; for then even if they are suspicious of you and talk against you, they will end up praising God for your good works when Christ returns.

13 For the Lord's sake, obey every law of your government: those of the king as head of the state,

14 And those of the king's officers, for he has sent them to punish all who do wrong, and to praise those who do right.

15 It is God's will that your good lives should silence those who foolishly condemn the Gospel with-

out knowing what it can do for them, having never experienced its power.

16 You are free from the law, but that doesn't mean you are free to do wrong. Live as those who are free to do only God's will at all times.

17 Show respect for everyone. Love Christians everywhere. Fear God and honor the government.

18 Servants, you must respect your masters and do whatever they tell you; not only if they are kind and reasonable, but even if they are tough and cruel.

19 Praise the Lord if you are punished for doing right!

20 Of course you get no credit for being patient if you are beaten for doing wrong; but if you do right and suffer for it, and are patient beneath the blows, God is well pleased.

21 This suffering is all part of the work God has given you; and Christ Who suffered for you is your example. Follow in His steps:

22 He never sinned, never told a lie,

23 Never answered back when insulted; when He suffered He did not threaten to get even; He left His case in the hands of God Who always judges fairly.

24 He personally carried the load of our sins in His own body when He died on the cross; so that we can be finished with sin, and live from now on for all that is good. For His wounds have healed ours!

25 Like sheep you wandered away from God, but now you have returned to your Shepherd, the Guardian of your souls Who keeps you safe from all attacks.

CHAPTER 3

Wives, fit in with your husband's plans; for then if they refuse to listen when you talk to them about the Lord, they will be won by your respectful, pure behavior; your godly lives will speak to them better than any words.

3 Don't be concerned about the outward beauty that depends on jewelry, or beautiful clothes, or hair arrangement.

4 Be beautiful inside, in your hearts, with the lasting charm of a gentle and quiet spirit which is so precious to God.

5 That kind of deep beauty was seen in the saintly women of old, who trusted God and fitted in with their husband's plans.

6 Sarah, for instance, obeyed her husband Abraham, honoring him as head of the house. And if you do the same, you will be following in her steps like good daughters and doing what is right; then you will not need to fear offending your husbands, nor the results of their decisions, nor their anger.†

7 You husbands must be careful of your wives, being thoughtful of their needs and honoring them as the weaker sex; remember that you and your wife are partners in receiving God's blessings together and if you don't treat her as you should, your prayers will not get ready answers.

8 And now this word to each of you: be as one big family, full of sympathy towards each other; full of love

†implied. The verse ends with the word "fear," without specifying of what.

for one another with tender hearts and humble minds.

9 Don't repay evil for evil. Don't snap back at those who say unkind things about you. Instead, pray for God's help for them, for we are to be kind to others, and God will bless us for it.

10 If you want a happy, good life, keep control of your tongue, and guard your lips from telling lies.

11 Turn away from evil and do good; try to live in peace even if you must run after it to catch and hold it!

12 For the Lord is watching His children, listening to their prayers; but the Lord's face is hard against those who do evil.

13 Usually no one will hurt you for wanting to do good.

14 But even if they should, you are to be envied, for God will reward you for it.

15 Quietly trust yourself to Christ your Lord and if anybody asks why you believe as you do, be ready to tell him and do it in a gentle and respectful way.

16 Do what is right; then, if men speak against you calling you evil names, they will become ashamed of themselves for falsely accusing you when you have only done what is good.

17 Remember, if God wants you to suffer, it is better to suffer for doing good than for doing wrong!

18 Christ also suffered. He died once for the sins of all us guilty sinners, although He Himself was innocent of any sin at any time, that He might bring us safely home to God. But though His body died, His spirit lived on,

19 And in it He visited the spirits in prison, and preached to them—

20 Spirits of those who, long before in the days of Noah, had refused to listen to God, though He waited patiently for them while Noah was building the ark. Yet only eight persons were saved from drowning in that terrible flood.

21 That, by the way, is what baptism pictures for us: in baptism we show that we have been saved from death and doom by the resurrection of Christ; not because our bodies are washed clean by the water, but because in being baptized we are turning to God and asking Him to cleanse our hearts from sin.

22 And now Christ is in heaven, sitting in the place of honor next to God the Father, with all the angels and powers of heaven bowing before Him and obeying Him.

CHAPTER 4

Since Christ had to suffer and undergo pain, we must have the same attitude He had; we must be ready to suffer too. For remember, when your body suffers, sin loses its power,

2 And you won't be spending the rest of your life chasing after evil desires, but will be anxious to do the will of God.

3 You have had enough in the past of the evil the godless enjoy—sex sin, lust, getting drunk, wild parties, drinking bouts, and the worship of idols—which leads to other terrible sins.

4 Of course your old friends will be very sur-

prised when you don't eagerly join them any more in the wicked things they do and they will laugh at you in contempt and scorn.

5 But just remember that they must face the Judge of all, living and dead; they will be judged for the way they have lived.

6 That is why the God News was preached even to those who were dead†—killed by the flood‡—so that although their bodies were punished with death, they could still live in their spirits as God lives.

7 The end of the world is coming soon. Therefore be earnest, thoughtful men of prayer.

8 Most important of all, continue to show deep love for each other, for love makes up for many of your faults.*

9 Cheerfully share your home with those who need a meal or a place to stay for the night.

10 God has given each of you some special abilities; be sure to use them to help each other, passing on to others God's many kinds of blessings.

11 Are you called to preach? Then preach as though God Himself were speaking through you. Are you called to help others? Do it with all the strength and energy that God supplies, so that God will be glori-

---

†Peter's meaning is unclear to all commentators. God's program for the unsaved today is "the wages of sin is death and after that the judgment." The Bible does not teach that those who are alive today will have a second chance to hear and accept the Gospel. For this reason some believe that verse 6 would be more accurately interpreted: "And that is why the Good News of salvation was preached (in their lifetime) to those who were going to die. For though their bodies would be given the death penalty, like anyone else, they could still be alive in the spirit, as God is."

‡implied. See I Peter 3:19, 20.

*Or, "love overlooks each other's many faults."

fied through Jesus Christ—to Him be glory and power forever and ever. Amen.

12 Dear friends, don't be bewildered or surprised when you go through the fiery trials ahead, for this is no strange, unusual thing that is going to happen to you.

13 Be full of joy, because these trials will make you partners with Christ in His suffering, and afterwards you will have the wonderful joy of sharing His glory in that coming day when it will be displayed.

14 Be happy if you are cursed and insulted for being a Christian, for when that happens the Spirit of God will come upon you with great glory.

15 Don't let me hear of your suffering for murdering or stealing or making trouble or being a busybody and prying into other people's affairs.

16 But it is no shame to suffer for being a Christian. Praise God for the privilege of being in Christ's family and being called by His wonderful name!

17 For the time has come for judgment, and it must begin first among God's own children. And if even we who are Christians must be judged, what terrible fate awaits those who have never believed in the Lord?

18 If the righteous are barely saved, what chance will the godless have?

19 So if you are suffering according to God's will, keep on doing what is right and trust yourself to the God Who made you, for He will never fail you.

CHAPTER 5

And now, a word to you elders of the church. I too am an elder; with my own eyes I saw Christ dying on the cross; and I too will share His glory and His honor when He returns. Fellow elders, this is my plea to you:

2 Feed the flock of God; care for it willingly, not grudgingly; not for what you will get out of it, but because you are eager to serve the Lord;

3 Don't be tyrants, but lead them by your good example,

4 And when the Head Shepherd comes, your reward will be a never-ending share in His glory and honor.

5 You younger men, follow the leadership of those who are older. And all of you serve each other with humble spirits, for God gives special blessings to those who are humble, but sets Himself against those who are proud.

6 Now is the time to humble yourselves under the mighty hand of God. In His good time He will lift you up.

7 Let Him have all your worries and cares, for He is always thinking about you and watching everything that concerns you.

8 Be careful, watch out for attacks from Satan, your great enemy. He prowls around like a hungry, roaring lion, looking for some victim to tear apart.

9 Stand firm when he attacks. Trust the Lord; and remember that other Christians all around the world are going through these sufferings too.

10 After you have suffered a little while, our God

Who is full of kindness through Christ will give you His eternal glory. He personally will come and pick you up, and set you firmly in place, and make you stronger than ever.

11 To Him be all power over all things, forever and ever. Amen.

12 I am sending this note to you through the courtesy of Silvanus who is, in my opinion, a very faithful brother. I hope I have encouraged you by this letter for I have given you a true statement of the way God blesses. Use this information to stand firmly in His love.

13 My wife† here in Rome—she is your sister in the Lord—sends you her greetings; so does my son Mark.

14 Give each other the handshake of Christian love. Peace be to all of you who are in Christ.

Peter

†literally: "She who is at Babylon, is likewise chosen;" but Babylon was the Christian nickname for Rome, and the "she" is thought by many to be Peter's wife to whom reference is made in Matthew 8:14, I Corinthians 9:5, etc. Others believe this should read "Your sister church here in Babylon salutes you, and so does my son Mark."

II Peter

CHAPTER 1

From: Simon Peter, a servant and missionary of Jesus Christ.

To: All of you who have our kind of faith. The faith I speak of is the kind that Jesus Christ our God and Saviour gives to us. How precious it is, and how just and good He is to give this same faith to each of us.

2 Do you want more and more of God's kindness and peace? Then learn to know Him better and better.

3 For as you know Him better, He will give you, through His great power, everything you need for living a truly good life: He even shares His own glory and His own goodness with us!

4 And by that same mighty power He has given us all the other rich and wonderful blessings He promised; for instance, the promise to save us from the lust and rottenness all around us, and to give us His own character.

5 But to obtain these gifts, you need more than faith; you must also work hard to be good, and even that is not enough. For then you must learn to know God better and discover what He wants you to do.

6 Next, learn to put aside your own desires so that you will become patient and godly, gladly letting God have His way.

7 This will make possible the next step, which is for

you to enjoy other people and to like them, and finally you will grow to love them deeply.

8 The more you go on in this way, the more you will grow strong spiritually and become fruitful and useful to our Lord Jesus Christ.

9 But anyone who fails to go after these additions to faith is blind indeed, or at least very shortsighted, and has forgotten that God delivered him from the old life of sin so that now he can live a strong, good life for the Lord.

10 So, dear brothers, work hard to prove that you really are among those God has called and chosen, and then you will never stumble or fall away.

11 And God will open wide the gates of heaven for you to enter in to the eternal kingdom of our Lord and Saviour Jesus Christ.

12 I plan to keep on reminding you of these things even though you already know them and are really getting along quite well!

13, 14 But the Lord Jesus Christ has showed me that my days are numbered here on earth, and I am soon to die. As long as I am still here I intend to keep sending these reminders to you,

15 Hoping to impress them so clearly upon you that you will remember them long after I have gone.

16 For we have not been telling you fairy tales when we explained to you the power of our Lord Jesus Christ and His coming again. My own eyes have seen His splendor and His glory:

17, 18 I was there on the holy mountain when He shone out with honor given Him by God His Father;

I heard that glorious, majestic voice calling down from heaven, saying, "This is my much-loved Son; I am well pleased with Him."

19 So we have seen and proved that what the prophets say comes true. You will do well to pay close attention to everything they have said, for, like lights shining into dark corners, their words help us to understand many things that otherwise would be dark and difficult. But when you consider the wonderful truth of the prophets' words, then the light will dawn in your souls and Christ the Morning Star will shine in your hearts.

20, 21 For no prophecy of Scripture was ever thought up by the prophet himself. For the Holy Spirit was within these men of God, giving them true messages from God.

CHAPTER 2

But there were false-prophets too in those days, just as there will be false teachers among you. They will cleverly tell their lies about God, turning against even their Master Who bought them; but theirs will be a swift and terrible end.

2 Many will follow their evil teaching that there is nothing wrong with sexual sin. And because of them Christ and His way will be scoffed at.

3 These teachers in their greed will tell you anything to get hold of your money. But God condemned them long ago and their destruction is on the way.

4 For God did not spare even the angels who sinned,

but threw them into hell, chained in gloomy caves and darkness until the judgment day.

5 And He did not spare any of the people who lived in olden times before the flood except Noah, the one man who spoke up for God, and his family of seven. At that time God completely destroyed the whole world of ungodly men with the vast flood.

6 Later, He turned the cities of Sodom and Gomorrah into heaps of ashes and blotted them off the face of the earth, making them an example for all the ungodly in the future to look back upon and fear.

7, 8 But at the same time the Lord rescued Lot out of Sodom because he was a good man, sick of the terrible wickedness he saw everywhere around him day after day.

9 So also the Lord can rescue you and me from the disasters He continues to use to punish the ungodly, until the day of final judgment comes.

10 He is especially hard on those who follow their own evil, lustful thoughts, and those who are proud and willful, daring even to scoff at the Glorious Ones without so much as trembling;

11 Although the angels in heaven who stand in the very presence of the Lord, and are far greater in power and strength than these false teachers, never speak out disrespectfully against these evil Mighty Ones.

12 But these false teachers are fools; like animals they do whatever they feel like; born only to be caught and killed, they laugh at the terrifying Powers of the Underworld which they know so little about; and they will be destroyed along with all the demons and powers of hell.

13 That is the pay these teachers will have for their sin. For they live in daily evil pleasures. They are a disgrace and a stain among you, deceiving you by living in foul sin on the side while they join your love feasts as though they were true men.

14 No woman can escape their sinful stare, and of adultery they never have enough. They make a game of luring unstable women. They train themselves to be greedy; and are doomed and cursed.

15 They have gone off the road and become lost like Balaam, the son of Beor, who fell in love with the money he could make by doing wrong;

16 But Balaam was stopped from his mad course when his donkey spoke to him with a human voice, scolding and rebuking him.

17 These men are useless as dried up springs of water, promising much and delivering nothing; they are unstable as clouds driven by the storm winds and are doomed to the eternal pits of darkness.

18 They are full of boasting about their sins and conquests, and using lust as their bait, they lure back into sin those who have just escaped from such wicked living.

19 "You aren't saved by being good," they say, "so you might as well be bad. Do what you like, be free." But these very teachers who offer this "freedom" from law are themselves slaves to sin and destruction. For a man is a slave to whatever controls him.

20 And when a person has escaped from the wicked ways of the world by learning about our Lord and Saviour Jesus Christ, and then gets tangled up with sin

and becomes its slave again, he is worse off than he was before.

21 It would be better if he had never known about Christ at all than to learn of Him and then afterwards turn his back on the holy commandments that were given to him.

22 There is an old saying that "A dog comes back to what he has vomited, and a pig is washed only to come back and wallow in the mud again." That is the way it is with those who turn again to their sin.

CHAPTER 3

This is my second letter to you, dear brothers, and in both of them I have tried to remind you—if you will let me—about facts you already know: facts you learned from the holy prophets and from us apostles who brought you the words of our Lord and Saviour.

3 First, I want to remind you that in the last days there will come scoffers who will do every wrong they can think of, and laugh at the truth.

4 This will be their line of argument: "So Jesus promised to come back, did He? Then where is He? He'll never come! Why, as far back as anyone can remember everything has remained exactly as it was since the first day of creation."

5, 6 They deliberately forget this fact: that God did destroy the world with a mighty flood, long after He had made the heavens by the word of His command, [illegible] had used the waters to form the earth and sur- [illegible] it.

7 And God has commanded that the earth and the heavens be stored away for a great bonfire at the judgment day, when all ungodly men will perish.

8 But don't forget this, dear friends, that a day or a thousand years from now is like tomorrow to the Lord.

9 So the Lord isn't being slow in coming as He promised, even though it sometimes seems that way. But He is waiting, for the good reason that He is not willing that any should perish, and He is giving more time for sinners to repent.

10 The day of the Lord is surely coming, as unexpectedly as a thief, and then the heavens will pass away with a terrible noise and the heavenly bodies will disappear in fire, and the earth and everything on it will be burned up.

11 And so since everything around us is going to melt away, what holy, godly lives we should be living!

12 You should look forward to that day and hurry it along—the day when God will set the heavens on fire, and the heavenly bodies will melt and disappear in flames.

13 But we are looking forward to God's promise of new heavens and a new earth afterwards, where only good will be.

14 Dear friends, while you are waiting for these things to happen and for Him to come, try hard to live without sinning; and be at peace with everyone so that He will be pleased with you when He returns.

15, 16 And remember why He is waiting. He is giving us time to get His message of salvation out to others. Our wise and beloved brother Paul has talked about these same things in many of his letters. Some of his comments are not easy to understand, and there are people who are deliberately stupid, and always demand some unusual interpretation; they have twisted his letters around to mean something quite different from what he meant, just as they do the other parts of the Scriptures, and the result is disaster for them.

17 I am warning you ahead of time, dear brothers, so that you can watch out and not be carried away by the mistakes of these wicked men, lest you yourselves become mixed up too.

18 But grow in spiritual strength and become better acquainted with our Lord and Saviour Jesus Christ. To Him be all glory and splendid honor, both now and forevermore. Amen.

Peter

I John

CHAPTER 1

Christ was alive when the world began, yet I myself have seen Him with my own eyes and listened to Him speak. I have touched Him with my own hands. He is God's message of Life.

2 This One Who is Life from God has been shown to us and we guarantee that we have seen Him; I am speaking of Christ, Who is eternal Life. He was with the Father and then was shown to us.

3 Again I say, we are telling you about what we ourselves have actually seen and heard, so that you may share the fellowship and the joys we have with the Father and with Jesus Christ His Son.

4 And if you do as I say in this letter, then you, too, will be full of joy, and so will we.

5 This is the message God has given us to pass on to you: That God is Light and in Him is no darkness at all.

6 So if we say we are His friends, but go on living in spiritual darkness and sin, we are lying.

7 But if we are living in the light of God's presence, just as Christ does, then we have wonderful fellowship and joy with each other, and the blood of Jesus His Son cleanses us from every sin.

8 If we say that we have no sin, we are only fooling ourselves, and refusing to accept the truth.

9 But if we confess our sins to Him, He can be depended on to forgive us our sins and to cleanse us from every wrong. And it is perfectly proper for God to do this for us because Christ died to wash away our sins.

10 If we claim we have not sinned, we are living and calling God a liar, *for He says we have sinned.*

CHAPTER 2

My little children, I am telling you this so that you will stay away from sin. But if you sin, there is Someone to plead for you before the Father. His name is Jesus Christ, the One Who is all that is good and Who pleases God completely.

2 He is the One Who took God's wrath against our sins upon Himself, and brought us into fellowship with God; and He is the forgiveness† for our sins, and not only ours but all the world's.

3 And how can we be sure that we belong to Him? By looking within ourselves: are we really trying to do what He wants us to?

4 Someone may say, "I am a Christian, I am on my way to heaven, I belong to Christ." But if he doesn't do what Christ tells him to, he is a liar.

5 But those who do what Christ tells them to will learn to love God more and more. That is the way to know whether or not you are a Christian.

†or, "atoning sacrifice"

6 Anyone who says he is a Christian should live as Christ did.

7 Dear brothers, I am not writing out a new rule for you to obey, for it is an old one you have always had, right from the start. You have heard it all before.

8 Yet it is always new, and it works for you just as it did for Christ; and as we obey this commandment, to love one another, the darkness in our lives disappears and the new light of life in Christ shines in.

9 Anyone who says he is walking in the light of Christ but hates his brother Christian is still in darkness.

10 But whoever loves his brother Christian is "walking in the light" and can see his way without stumbling around in darkness and sin.

11 But he who hates his Christian brother is wandering around in spiritual darkness, and doesn't know where he is going, for the darkness has made him blind so that he cannot see the way.

12 I am writing these things to all of you, my little children, because your sins have been forgiven in the name of Jesus our Saviour.

13 I am saying these things to you older men because you really know Christ, the One Who has been alive from the beginning. And you young men, I am talking to you because you have won your battle with Satan. And I am writing to you younger boys and girls because you, too, have learned to know God our Father.

14 And so I say to you fathers who know the eternal God, and to you young men who are strong, with God's word in your hearts, and have won your battles against Satan:

15 Stop loving this evil world and all that it offers you, for when you love these things you show that you do not really love God;

16 For all these worldly things, these evil desires—the craze for sex, the ambition to buy everything that appeals to you and the pride that comes from wealth and importance—these are not from God. They are from this evil world itself.

17 And this world is fading away, and these evil, forbidden things will go with it, but whoever keeps doing the will of God will remain forever.

18 Dear children, this world's last hour has come. You have heard about the Anti-Christ who is coming—the one who is against Christ—and already many such persons have appeared. This makes us all the more certain that the end of the world is near.

19 These "against-Christ" people used to be members of our churches but they never really belonged with us, or else they would have stayed. When they left us it proved that they didn't belong.

20 But you are not like that, for the Holy Spirit has come upon you, and you know the truth.

21 So I am not writing to tell you anything new, but because you know the truth and the difference between truth and falsehood.

22 Who is the greatest liar? He is the one who says that Jesus is not Christ. He is "anti-Christ" who does not believe in God the Father and His Son.

23 For a person who doesn't believe in Christ, God's Son, can't have God the Father either. But he who has Christ, God's Son, has God the Father too.

24 So keep on believing what you have been taught from the beginning. If you do, then you will always be in close fellowship with both God the Father and His Son.

25 And He Himself has promised us this: *eternal life*.

26 These remarks of mine about the "anti-Christ" are pointed at those who would dearly love to blindfold you and lead you astray.

27 But you have received the Holy Spirit and He lives within you, in your hearts, so that you don't need anyone to teach you what is right. For He teaches you all things, and He is the Truth, and no liar; and so, just as He has said, you must live in Christ, never to depart from Him.

28 And now, my little children, stay in happy fellowship with the Lord so that when He comes you will be sure that all is well, and not have to be ashamed, and shrink back from meeting Him.

29 Since we know that God is always good and does only right, then we can expect that all those who do right are His children.

CHAPTER 3

See how very much our heavenly Father loves us, for He allows us to be called His children—think of it—and we really *are*. But since most people don't know God, naturally they don't understand that we are His children.

2 Yes, dear friends, we are already God's children,

right now, and we can't even imagine what it is going to be like later on. But we do know this, that when He comes we will be like Him, as a result of seeing Him as He really is.

3 And everyone who really believes this will try to stay pure because Christ is pure.

4 But those who keep on sinning are against God, for every sin is done against the will of God.

5 And you know that He became a man so that He could take away our sins, and that there is no sin in Him, no missing of God's will at any time in any way.

6 So if we stay close to Him, obedient to Him, we won't be sinning either; but those who keep on sinning should realize this: they sin because they have never really known Him and become His.

7 Oh, dear people, don't let anyone deceive you about this: if you are constantly doing what is good, it is because you *are* good, even as He is.

8 But if you keep on sinning, it shows that you belong to Satan, who since he first began to sin has kept steadily at it. But the Son of God came to destroy these works of the devil.

9 The person who has been born into God's family does not make a practice of sinning because now God's life is in him, and so he can't keep on sinning, for this new life has been born into him and controls him—he has been born again.

10 So now we can tell who is a child of God and who belongs to Satan. Whoever is living a life of sin and doesn't love his brother shows that he is not in God's family.

11 For the message to us from the beginning has been that we should love one another.

12 We are not to be like Cain, who belonged to Satan and killed his brother. Why did he kill him? Because Cain had been doing wrong and he knew very well that his brother's life was better than his.

13 So don't be surprised, dear friends, if the world hates you.

14 If we love other Christians it proves that we have been delivered from hell and given eternal life in heaven. But a person who doesn't have love for others is headed for eternal death.

15 Anyone who hates his Christian brother is really a murderer at heart; and you know that no one wanting to murder has eternal life within.

16 We know what real love is from Christ's example, dying for us. And so we ought to lay down our lives for our Christian brothers.

17 But if someone who is supposed to be a Christian has money enough to live well, and sees a brother in need, and won't help him—how can God's love be within *him?*

18 Little children, let us stop just *saying* we love people; let us *really* love them, and *show it* by our *actions.*

19 Then we will know for sure, by our actions, that we are on God's side and our consciences will be clear, even when we stand before the Lord.

20 But if we have bad consciences and feel that we have done wrong, the Lord will surely feel that way about us even more, for He knows everything we do.

21 But, dearly loved friends, if our consciences are clear, we can come to the Lord with perfect assurance and trust,

22 And get whatever we ask for because we are obeying Him and doing the things that please Him well.

23 And this is what God says we must do: believe on the name of His Son Jesus Christ, and love one another.

24 Those who do what God says—they are living with God and He with them. We know this is true because the Holy Spirit He has given us tells us so.

CHAPTER 4

Dearly loved friends, don't always believe everything you hear just because someone says it is a message from God: test it first to see if it really is. For there are many false teachers around.

2 This is the way to find out if the message is from the Holy Spirit: Does it really agree that Jesus Christ, God's Son, actually became man with a human body? If so, then the message is from God.

3 If not, the message is not from God but from one who is against Christ, like the "Anti-Christ" you have heard about who is going to come, and his attitude of enmity against Christ is already abroad in the world.

4 Dear young friends, you belong to God and have already won your fight with those who are against Christ, because there is Someone in your hearts Who is stronger than any evil teacher in this wicked world.

5 These men belong to this world, so, quite

naturally, they are concerned about worldly affairs and the world pays attention to them.

6 But we are children of God, and so only those who have walked and talked with God will listen to us. Others won't. That is another way to know whether a message is really from God; for if it is, the world won't listen to it.

7 Dear friends, let us practice loving each other, for love comes from God and those who are loving and kind show that they are the children of God, and that they are getting to know Him better.

8 But if a person isn't loving and kind, it shows that he doesn't know God. For God is love.

9 God showed how much He loved us by sending His only Son down from heaven to bring to us eternal life through His death.

10 So now we know what real love is: it is not our love for God, but His love for us when He sent His Son to satisfy God's anger against our sins.

11 Dear friends, since God loved us as much as that, we surely ought to love each other too.

12 For though we have never yet seen God, when we love each other God lives in us and His love within us grows ever stronger.

13 And He has put His own Holy Spirit into our hearts as a proof to us that we are living with Him and He with us.

14 And I have seen with my own eyes and now tell all the world that God sent His Son to be their Saviour.

15 Anyone who believes and says that Jesus is the

Son of God, God is living in that person and that person is living with God.

16 We know how much God loves us because we have felt His love and because we believe Him when He tells us that He loves us dearly. God is love, and anyone who lives in love is living with God and God is living in Him.

17 And as we live with Christ, our love grows more perfect and complete; and so we will not be ashamed and embarrassed at the day of judgment, but can face Him with confidence and joy, because He loves us and we love Him too.

18 We need have no fear of Someone Who loves us perfectly; His perfect love for us eliminates all dread of what He might do to us. If we are afraid, it is for fear of what He might do to us, and shows that we are not fully convinced that He really loves us.

19 So you see, our love for Him comes as a result of His loving us first.

20 If anyone says, "I love God," but keeps on hating his brother, he is a liar; for if he doesn't love his brother who is right there in front of him how can he love God Whom he has never seen?

21 And God Himself has said that one must not only love God, but his brother too.

CHAPTER 5

If you believe that Jesus is the Christ—that He is God's Son and your Saviour—then you are a child of God. And all who love the Father love His children too.

2 So you can find out how much you love God's children—your brothers and sisters in the Lord—by how much you love and obey God.

3 Loving God means doing what He tells us to, and really that isn't hard at all,

4 For every child of God can obey Him, defeating sin and evil pleasure by trusting Christ to help him.

5 But who could possibly fight and win this battle except by believing that Jesus is truly the Son of God?

6-8 And we know He is because God said so with a voice from heaven when Jesus was baptized, and again as He was facing death.† It spoke not only at His baptism but also as He faced death.§ And the Holy Spirit, forever truthful, says it too. So we have these three witnesses: the Holy Spirit, and the voice from heaven at Christ's baptism, and the voice before He died.* And they all say the same thing: that Jesus Christ is the Son of God.‡

9 We use men as witnesses in our courts, and so we can surely believe what God tells us. And God has said that Jesus is His Son.

10 All who believe this know in their hearts that it is true. If anyone doesn't believe this, he is actually calling God a liar, because he doesn't believe what God has said about His Son.

11 And what is it God has said? That He has given us eternal life, and that this life is in His Son.

---

†literallly, "This is He who came by water and blood." See Matthew 3:16, 17; Luke 9:31, 35; John 12:27, 28, 32, 33. Other interpretations of this verse are equally possible.

§literally, "not by water only, but by water and blood."

*literally, "the Spirit, and the water, and the blood."

‡implied

12 So whoever has God's Son has life; whoever does not have His Son, does not have life.

13 I have written this to you who believe in the Son of God so that you may know you have eternal life.

14 And we are sure of this, that He will listen to us whenever we ask Him for anything in line with His will.

15 And if we really know He is listening when we talk to Him and make our requests, then we can be sure that He will answer us.

16 If you see a Christian sinning in a way that does not end in death, you should ask God to forgive him and God will give him life, unless he has sinned that one fatal sin. But there is that one sin which ends in death and if he has done that, there is no use praying for him.

17 Every wrong is a sin, of course. I'm not talking about these ordinary sins; I am speaking of that one that ends in death.†

18 No one who has become part of God's family makes a practice of sinning, for Christ, God's Son, holds him securely and the devil cannot get his hands on him.

19 We know that we are children of God and that all the rest of the world around us is under Satan's power and control.

20 And we know that Christ, God's Son, has come

---

†Commentators differ widely in their thoughts about what sin this is, and whether it causes physical death or spiritual death. Blasphemy against the Holy Spirit results in spiritual death (Mark 3:29) but can a Christian ever sin in such a way? Impenitence at the Communion Table sometimes ends in physical death (I Cor. 11:30). And Hebrews 6:4-8 speaks of the terrible end of those who fall away.

to help us understand and find the true God. And now we are in God because we are in Jesus Christ His Son, Who is the only true God; and He is eternal Life.

21 Dear children, keep away from anything that might take God's place in your hearts. Amen.

John

II John

From: John, the old Elder of the church.

To: That dear woman Cyria, one of God's very own, and to her children whom I love so much, as does everyone else in the church.

2 Since the Truth is in our hearts forever,

3 God the Father and Jesus Christ His Son will bless us with great mercy and much peace, with truth and love.

4 How happy I am to find some of your children here, and to see that they are living as they should, following the Truth, obeying God's commands.

5 And now I want to urgently remind you, dear friends, of the old rule God gave us right from the beginning, that Christians should love one another.

6 If we love God, we will do whatever He tells us to. And He has told us from the very first to love each other.

7 Watch out for the false leaders—and there are many of them around—who don't believe that Jesus Christ came to earth as a human being with a body like ours. Such people are against the truth and against Christ.

8 Beware of being like them, and losing the prize that you and I have been working so hard to get. See to it that you win your full reward from the Lord.

9 For if you wander away from the teaching of

Christ, you will lose God; while if you are loyal to Christ's teachings, you will have God too. Then you will have both the Father and the Son.

10 If anyone comes to teach you, and he doesn't believe what Christ taught, don't even invite him into your home. Don't encourage him in any way.

11 If you do, you will be a partner with him in his wickedness.

12 Well I would like to say much more, but I don't want to say it in this letter for I hope to come to see you soon and then we can talk over these things together and have a joyous time.

13 Greetings from the children of your sister—another choice child of God.

John

III John

From: John, the Elder.
To: Dear Gaius, whom I truly love.

2 Dear friend, I am praying that all will go well with you and that your body will be as healthy as I know your soul is;

3 For some of the traveling brothers who come here have made me very happy by telling me that your life is clean and true, and that you are living by the standards of the Gospel.

4 I could have no greater joy than to hear such things about my children.

5 Dear friend, you are doing a good work for God in taking care of the traveling teachers and missionaries who are passing through.

6 They have told the church here of your friendship and your loving deeds. I am glad when you send them on their way with a generous gift.

7 For they are traveling for the Lord, and take neither food, clothing, shelter or money from those who are not Christians, even though they have preached to them.

8 So we ourselves should take care of them in order that we may become partners with them in the Lord's work.

9 I sent a brief letter to the church about this, but proud Diotrephes, who loves to push himself forward as

the leader of the Christians there, does not admit my authority over him and refuses to listen to me.

10 When I come I will tell you some of the things he is doing and what wicked things he is saying about me and what insulting language he is using. He not only refuses to welcome the missionary travelers himself, but tells others not to, and when they do he tries to put them out of the church.

11 Dear friend, don't let this bad example influence you. Only follow what is good. Remember that those who do what is right prove that they are God's children; and those who continue in evil prove that they are far from God.

12 But everyone, including Truth itself, speaks highly of Demetrius. I myself can say the same for him, and you know I speak the truth.

13 I have much to say but I don't want to write it,

14 For I hope to get there soon and then we will have much to talk about together.

15 So good-bye for now. Friends here send their love, and please give each of the folks there a special greeting from me.

John

Jude

From: Jude, a servant of Jesus Christ, and a brother of James.

To: Christians everywhere, for God the Father has chosen you and kept you for Jesus Christ.

2 May you be given more and more of God's kindness, peace, and love.

3 Dearly loved friends, I had been planning to write you some thoughts about the salvation God has given us, but now I find I must write of something else instead, urging you to stoutly defend the truth which God gave, once for all, to His people to keep without change through the years.

4 I say this because some godless teachers have wormed their way in among you saying after we become Christians we can do just as we like without fear of God's punishment. The fate of such people was written long ago, for they have turned against our only Master and Lord, Jesus Christ.

5 My answer to them is: remember this fact—which you know already—that the Lord saved a whole nation of people out of the land of Egypt, and then killed every one of them who did not trust and obey Him.

6 And I remind you of those angels who were once pure and holy, but willingly turned to a life of sin. Now

God has them chained up in prisons of darkness, waiting for the judgment day.

7 And don't forget the cities of Sodom and Gomorrah and their neighboring towns, all full of lust of every kind including lust of men for other men. Those cities were destroyed by fire and continue to be a warning to us that there is a hell in which sinners are punished.

8 Yet these false teachers go on living their evil immoral lives, degrading their bodies and laughing at those in authority over them, even scoffing at the glorious ones—those mighty powers of awful evil who left their first estate.

9 Even Michael, one of the mightiest of the angels, when he was arguing with Satan about Moses' body, did not dare to accuse Satan, or jeer at him, but simply said, "The Lord rebuke you."

10 But these men mock and curse at anything they do not understand, and, like animals, they do whatever they feel like, thereby ruining their souls.

11 Woe upon them! For they follow the example of Cain who killed his brother; and, like Balaam, they will do anything for money; and, like Korah, they have disobeyed God in the hope of gain and will die under His curse.

12 When these men join you at the love feasts of the church, they are evil smears among you, laughing and carrying on, gorging and stuffing themselves without a thought for others. They are like clouds blowing over dry land without giving rain, promising much, but producing nothing. They are like fruit trees without any fruit at picking time. They are not only dead, but

doubly dead, for they have been pulled out roots and all for burning.

13 All they leave behind them is shame and disgrace like the dirty foam along the beach left by the wild waves. They wander around looking as bright as stars, but ahead of them is everlasting gloom and darkness that God has ready for them.

14 Enoch, who lived long ago soon after Adam, knew about these men and said this about them: "See, the Lord is going to come with millions of His people;

15 "He will bring the people of the world before Him in judgment, to receive just punishment, and to prove the terrible things they have done in rebellion against God, revealing all they have said against Him."

16 These men are constant gripers, never satisfied, doing whatever evil they feel like; they are loud-mouthed "show-offs," and when they show respect for others, it is only to get something from them in return.

17 Dear friends, remember what the apostles of our Lord Jesus Christ told you,

18 That in the last times there would come these scoffers whose whole purpose in life is to enjoy themselves in every evil way imaginable.

19 They stir up arguments; they love the evil things of the world; they do not have the Holy Spirit living in them.

20 But you, dear friends, must build up your lives ever more strongly upon the foundation of our holy faith, learning to pray in the power and strength of the Holy Spirit.

21 Stay always within the boundaries where God's

love can reach and bless you. Wait patiently for the eternal life that our Lord Jesus Christ in His mercy is going to give you.

22 Try to help those who argue against you. Be merciful to those who doubt.

23 Save some by snatching them as from the very flames of hell itself. And as for others, help them to find the Lord by being kind to them, but fear the possibility of being pulled along into their sins. Hate every trace of their sin while being merciful to them as sinners.

24, 25 And now—glory to Him Who alone is God, Who saves us through Jesus Christ our Lord; yes, splendor and majesty, all power and authority are His from the beginning; His they are and His they evermore will be. And He is able to keep you from slipping and falling away, and to bring you, sinless and perfect, into His glorious presence with mighty shouts of everlasting joy. AMEN.